Contents

Foreword

The NEBOSH HSE Certificate in Process Safety Management is the perfect qualification for those who need to understand the principles of process safety management as part of their job. By studying for this qualification you will be able to contribute to the effective management of process safety and be able to profile the major risks present in a typical process installation.

The qualification is particularly relevant to the following people working within a process environment:

• Team leaders, supervisors and managers

• Process operators

• Newly qualified health and safety advisors

The qualification is not designed for chemical and process safety engineers experienced in the specification, design and maintenance of the integrity of process plant.

This course book has been structured to match the NEBOSH syllabus. It has been written by process safety experts, who take you step-by-step through the content of the qualification. The information is divided into distinct sections, each of which starts by listing the learning outcomes for that particular section. It isn't full of jargon or confusing terms and offers useful examples, mock exam questions and helpful tips throughout to aid your learning.

Using this book as part of your course preparation and study could improve your chance of success. How you use this book is entirely up to you however, we would definitely recommend that you use it as a revision aid as part of your formal course leading to the qualification. You may feel you want to read it from cover to cover, or you may simply want to read certain chapters where you would like to concentrate your studies. You will also find it useful as a source of reference when you are back in your workplace.

The NEBOSH HSE Certificate in Process Safety Management is intended to be suitable for students working anywhere in the world. The content is based on recognised international best practice. Knowledge of specific legislation, either in the UK or in any other country, is not a requirement of the qualification.

Further information, including the Guide for the qualification can be found on the NEBOSH website at www.nebosh.org.uk.

The NEBOSH HSE Certificate in Process Safety Management also complements other NEBOSH qualifications such as the NEBOSH National or International General Certificate in Occupational Health and Safety.

We hope you find this book useful and thank you for taking the time to learn more about process safety management.

A guide to the symbols used in this course book

THOUGHT PROVOKER

These ask you to think about what you have been learning, to relate it to your own experience.

ACTIVITY

Carry out an activity to reinforce what you have just read.

EXAMPLE

Real or imagined scenarios that give context to points made in the text.

KEY TERMS

Definitions of key process safety terminology.

Element 1 **Process safety leadership**

Process safety leadership

HSE inspectors inspect an offshore oil platform.
©*Crown Copyright, Health and Safety Executive*

This element will explore what process safety is and will look at the importance of leadership in the process industries. It will also introduce organisational learning, management of change, and how worker engagement can be managed.

Learning outcomes

On completion of this element, you should be able to:

1.1 Outline the meaning of process safety and how it differs from personal safety.

1.2 Explain the role of leadership in process safety management.

1.3 Explain the purpose of organisational learning, the sharing of lessons learnt and sources of information.

1.4 Explain how 'change' should be managed to effectively reduce risks to people and plant.

1.5 Outline the benefits, limitations and types of worker participation and engagement.

1.6 Outline what is meant by competence and its importance to process safety.

Process safety management meaning

1. The distinction between process safety vs personal safety

When we think about 'safety', we naturally think about the personal safety of individuals who could be affected, and the various, often more traditional actions that can be taken to reduce the risk of injury and ill health. Many types of personal accidents are quite common, simple and therefore reasonably foreseeable; their control measures are often well established and straightforward to implement. These include machine guarding, fire precautions, equipment checks, managing slips and trips and the use of personal protective equipment (PPE). We probably think about low personal accident rates or number of days without an accident as a measure of success.

By comparison, process safety (safety in high-hazard process industries) is rather more complicated. So-called high-hazard process industries include chemical and oil and gas sectors. While they obviously suffer personal accidents like all other workplaces, there is also the potential for a major incident. This is because they deal with dangerous chemicals in large amounts and operate processes that, if not well monitored and controlled, can easily go spectacularly wrong, resulting in major fires and toxic releases, for example. Major incidents like these are very infrequent events and can be difficult to predict (before they happen) because of the multiple causes and complexity of what leads to them. Neglecting seemingly small things (like an intermittently faulty alarm or general maintenance) can end up causing a major accident. In process safety, the emphasis is on the prevention of major disasters that have been historically an issue for the industry. Process safety needs both complex technical controls (on the plant itself) as well as a robust safety management system. It requires a good deal of specialist technical engineering and management skill to get right. Leadership is important to give suitable high priority to process safety even though the standards and controls mean that incidents should be rare and may be outside the experience of operators.

Personal safety and process safety do link together (clearly, there is a risk of slips, trips and falls occurring in any workplace); however, in process safety, the emphasis is on the prevention of the high-risk, large scale catastrophic events that, though thankfully rare, could have devastating consequences.

2. A definition of process safety

You will find various definitions of process safety but the one that we will use here is: "a blend of engineering and management skills focused on preventing catastrophic accidents and near misses, particularly structural collapse, explosions, fires and toxic releases associated with loss of containment of energy or dangerous substances such as chemicals and petroleum products." (Energy Institute, adapted from the Center for Chemical Process Safety of the American Institute of Chemical Engineers[1]).

As you can see, it has all the elements of what we have discussed earlier.

St. Fergus gas terminal, Scotland.
©Crown Copyright, Health and Safety Executive

Process safety leadership

There have been a number of incidents in the process industry that have called into question the way that safety is managed; specifically, in relation to inadequate leadership and poor organisational culture.

EXAMPLE

Focus has historically been on the engineering solutions and design improvements that could be made; however, the hydrocarbon explosions at Texas City and Buncefield in 2005, as well as the more recent Macondo blowout (explosion of BP's Deepwater Horizon offshore drilling unit) highlighted the need to focus on not only the physical controls but also the leadership actions that will prevent such events. As a result, in the UK the Process Safety Leadership Group (PSLG) was established in 2007 to work with the regulators in order to form guidelines on the management and leadership actions that are needed.

In the PSLG final report[2] into the Buncefield disaster, the importance of leadership was acknowledged. Appendix 7 of that document contains their "Principles of Process Safety Leadership[2]", which we will broadly cover in this section.

ACTIVITY

We will be discussing Buncefield at several points through the element, so it would be useful for you to be aware of the incident. The report into the HSE's prosecution of companies involved in the Buncefield explosion, together with photographs and video evidence, can be viewed on the HSE's website (at www.hse.gov.uk/news/buncefield at the time of writing.) Review some of the evidence and familiarise yourself with the case.

1. Hazard and risk awareness of leadership teams

Leaders need to be competent and actively engaged. Indeed, the earlier referenced PSLG report states that "at least one board member should be fully conversant in process safety management in order to advise the board of the status of process safety risk management within the organisation and of the process safety implications of board decisions".

History has shown that if process industry leaders do not fundamentally understand the hazards and risks inherent in their business, unless they are extremely lucky, ignorance may ultimately lead to disaster. Lack of understanding may arise from things such as lack of technical knowledge or simply lack of data on which to base a decision (lack of reporting). Leadership teams are key decision-makers. If, through ignorance, they do not fully appreciate the consequences of their decisions (such as delaying plant maintenance on an already elderly plant or cutting critical staff), they will make poor decisions that may make a major accident inevitable (just a matter of time). To appreciate this, leaders need to be involved, competent and actively engaged - it does not happen by chance. They need to be fully aware of the hazard and risk potential of their processing activities and the potential consequences that decisions to do (or not do) things may lead to. Though a major incident may never have happened to the organisation in question, the major accident potential of its processes needs to be treated seriously alongside other business risks, since it is far more likely to have an impact on reputation and the survival of the business as a whole.

After effects of the fire at Buncefield oil storage facility.
©*Crown Copyright, Health and Safety Executive*

Process safety leadership

Clearly, leadership teams must therefore be aware of the hazards and potential impacts of their plant and sites (at every stage of their life cycle, from design to decommissioning). These impacts could not only result in life-threatening safety events but also reputational damage and business losses.

THOUGHT PROVOKER

Consider the organisation or environment that you work in - how confident are you that leaders and managers are fully aware of the hazard potentials of the process?

EXAMPLE

In the 1988 Piper Alpha oil rig disaster, 167 lives were lost, insured losses reached £1.7 billion and impacted 10% of North Sea oil and gas production. Nearly 30 years on, the name "Piper Alpha" symbolises a monumental failure of process safety and the reputation of the Occidental organisation was tarnished forever.

ACTIVITY

Piper Alpha will be discussed several times in the course, so it would be useful to have an understanding of the disaster. Use the HSE website, search engines and public access video sites to understand (in no great detail) what happened and why the incident had such a profound impact on the industry and process safety as a whole.

Further, they of course need to understand the criticality of the layers of preventive and protective measures that prevent, detect and mitigate such undesirable events.

For those board members still unsure as to the importance of managing process safety, the publication Corporate Governance for Process Safety - Guidance for Senior Leaders in High Hazard Industries[3] contains the following statement:

"Safe operation and sustainable success in business cannot be separated. Failure to manage process safety can never deliver good performance in the long term, and the consequences of getting control of major hazards wrong are extremely costly... Major accidents may not just impact on your bottom line profitability - they could completely wipe it out. Major incidents in recent years have shown that the consequences for capital costs, income, insurance costs, investment confidence and shareholder value can all be drastically affected. So why take the risk? However, getting it right pays large dividends."

2. Board level visibility and promotion of process safety leadership

The Principles of Process Safety Leadership also place emphasis on board level visibility to promote process safety.

Directors and senior managers play a key role in promotion of process safety - they provide leadership, set direction and assign priorities, establish the health and safety 'tone' of the organisation and ensure that the organisation's legal responsibilities are met.

As such, their actions are noted by workers and their visible leadership is essential in the development of the safety culture of the organisation. Of course, leaders need to reinforce personal safety, such as wearing PPE, but also need to discuss and question the more complex issues such as resourcing and the process operations. The actions taken at leadership level establish the level of commitment to process safety which, in turn, helps to achieve the desired positive health and safety culture. Part of being visible is personally leading initiatives, challenging the organisation (asking difficult questions) and actually being physically present (visiting sites). In short, they need to be role models.

Process safety responsibilities need to be defined.
©Crown Copyright, Health and Safety Executive

3. The need to define process safety responsibilities

It is not only directors who have a role to play in process safety. Top management will delegate (even though they will retain overall responsibility and accountability) to their subordinates. So, other managers and workers will also have process safety critical roles and responsibilities as part of their duties. Obviously, such responsibilities should only be delegated to those who are competent to carry them out (or where that competence is actively being developed). These should be clearly defined at all levels; from the board through to the maintenance workers who look after the installation, everyone has a role to play in process safety. This is especially so for those with Process Safety Management (PSM) critical positions. For example, the engineering manager may be responsible for the management of change process, which ensures that modifications to plant or process are carried out only after consideration of the safety implications; the maintenance manager may have accountability for the development and implementation of the preventive maintenance and breakdown strategies, while the engineers, electricians and fitters may be responsible for contributing to the risk assessments and following the permit-to-work process and locking off equipment before work commences.

THOUGHT PROVOKER

How confident are you that you understand your process safety responsibilities? What about your colleagues and senior managers?

4. The reasons for holding to account all individuals with PSM responsibility

It is clear that if new plant is installed without due consideration to safety, then the potential for injuries is high, eg if everything is correct and an electrician simply takes shortcuts and does not isolate the system before work, the potential for injury is also high. Everyone with process safety responsibilities has a role to play and therefore should be held accountable for their actions, regardless of their organisational level. In the context of an adequately resourced, competent workforce, holding people accountable also encourages engagement. However, it is very important for process safety to look for root causes of incidents rather than blaming an individual. Root cause analysis finds wider failings in the systems, management and leadership. Also, in the example above, a 'just' culture would encourage the electrician to report near misses and contribute to the development of safer working systems, without fear that a single mistake will lead to disciplinary action or even sacking. So, we might ask ourselves how such a culture is created, the answer is simple; senior managers play a pivotal role. Senior managers set the standards for the design of plant, the operational standards that are acceptable and conversely reinforce the fact that corner cutting and taking shortcuts is totally unacceptable in process safety. Effective senior managers dedicate resources to safety rather than paying lip service to it, and ensure that true root causes are identified after incidents. This theme is returned to under 'Organisational Learning' below.

In the previously referenced Corporate Governance for Process Safety - Guidance for Senior Leaders in High Hazard Industries publication, the following suggestions are made with regard to organisational competence and responsibility. CEOs and leaders assure their organisation's competence to manage the hazards of its operations; they:

- understand which questions to ask their workers and know which follow-up actions are necessary;

- ensure there are competent management, engineering, and operational workers at all levels;

- ensure continual development of process safety expertise and learning from new regulation and guidance;

- provide resources and time for expertise-based hazard and risk analyses, effective training and comprehensive scenario-planning for potential accidents.

Process safety leadership

- defer to the expertise of personnel, and do not dismiss expert opinions. They provide a process or system to ensure company leaders get expert process safety input as a critical part of the decision making process for commercial projects or activities;

- ensure that the organisation monitors and reviews the process safety competency of contractors and third parties;

- are capable of openly communicating critical aspects of process safety with all internal and external audiences.

5. The provision of adequate resources

Process safety needs to be adequately resourced; ensuring adequate resources are in place is the responsibility of the leadership of the organisation. Again, returning to the PSLG leadership principles, we find the following: "Appropriate resources should be made available to ensure a high standard of process safety management throughout the organisation and staff with process safety responsibilities should have or develop an appropriate level of competence." These resources can be:

- human - the right number of people with the right skills and experiences;

- financial - this may include capital expenditure and operational budgets to allow the plant to operate safely;

- physical - such as equipment, buildings, offices, rest facilities, etc.

Under-resourcing process safety is a risky business. While it may be unreasonable to expect an unlimited budget or unlimited pool of personnel to draw on, it is entirely reasonable to expect a high-risk process operator to take its responsibilities seriously. The impacts of a process safety incident can be catastrophic - in September 2001, an explosion in the AZF fertiliser factory in Toulouse, France resulted in 29 deaths, 30 serious injuries and 2,500 other casualties. Total compensation paid by the insurance group exceeded 1.5 billion Euros. As well as the financial implications of such failures, there are huge moral expectations placed on employers, which was clear after the Deepwater Horizon explosion in 2012 that saw the chair of BP in the spotlight for the organisation's failings and huge public backlash. There are also legal implications in many countries that place accountability clearly at the feet of the leaders to ensure safety (including process safety) is adequately managed.

6. Reasons for establishing process safety objectives and targets

There is an old adage that states "if you aren't measuring, you aren't managing" and this is as true for the process industry sector as it is for any other. The meaning of process safety objectives and targets is that effective organisations, serious about making safety improvements, will establish a clear set of objectives (overarching process safety aims) and targets (short term goals) that are cascaded to staff throughout the organisation at all levels. Leading and lagging process safety indicators (things that you would measure to indicate progress towards your objectives and targets) should be established in order to take the organisation towards its goal. We will discuss these indicators in the context of a process safety management system in Element 2.

There are sound reasons for establishing effective process safety objectives, targets and indicators. An organisation could adopt a 'wait and see' approach to safety management, assuming that 'no news is good news'. However, a lack of incidents is no guarantee of safety, it could be the result of good old-fashioned luck. Effective process safety indicators identify safety critical controls and actions, and monitor these to ensure that operations are running as intended, controls are robust and the site is therefore under control.

Once these safety indicators and targets have been established, the board should review progress on a regular basis (often quarterly) and, on an annual basis, the performance against these targets should be published in order to celebrate success and highlight areas of opportunity. For many organisations (such as those appearing on the London Stock Exchange), this will be included in the annual report to shareholders and therefore is publicly available.

ACTIVITY

Identify three process safety indicators that are used in your workplace to monitor process safety. Write these down, as we will come back to them in Element 2.

7. Commitment to continuous improvement

Leaders should not only actively and effectively monitor the safety performance; they should also seek to continually improve, eg by benchmarking against other organisations.

Ultimately, process safety, like the personal safety we explored at the start of this element, is a never-ending story. Organisations develop, plants change and the desire for further safety improvements is therefore a continual process, rather than being disheartening, this is enlightening as it acknowledges that the best organisations strive continually for the injury-free workplace or the incident-free plant and acknowledge that it is achievable with the right level of commitment.

HSE inspectors discussing work carried out on a chemical plant.
©*Crown Copyright, Health and Safety Executive*

Organisational learning

Individuals learn from mistakes throughout their lives but organisations frequently repeat the same mistakes they made decades before (this is commonly referred to as 'corporate amnesia'). In this section, we will look at why this is so important in process safety and how to ensure organisations learn.

1. The significance of learning lessons from incidences of actual or potential consequence

Major incidents cannot easily be ignored - they create an awful lot of damage. As an organisation (or even as an individual), it is tempting to play down the significance of a near miss that could have led to a major incident (but was caught in time and averted). For example, if a process line ruptures during a nightshift and chemical is sprayed into an empty area of the plant, it is easy to categorise this as a 'near miss' or 'environmental release' - but if the plant simply breathes a collective sigh of relief and ignores the true potential, then the root cause may not be fully identified and the wrong level of response may be given.

When incidents happen to other similar plants or organisations (rather than to you), there is a tendency to be complacent and think it could never happen to you (simply based on the idea that it has not so far and therefore you must be doing it all right). But, you might just have been lucky. If you fail to investigate and learn lessons (of how to do things differently), the danger is that the very same issue will repeat and next week, next month or next year, you will not be so lucky.

THOUGHT PROVOKER

Think of a recent process safety incident that has occurred in your workplace that did not result in injury (a spill, loss of containment, etc). How was the investigation managed? Was it investigated briefly as a 'near miss' or was it viewed as having the potential for a more serious event and investigated more stringently?

2. The reasons for and benefits of accident and incident investigation

Incidents happen in all workplaces, and the process industry is no different. While hopefully major incidents and disasters are few and far between, the need to investigate and address the causes of the minor events should not be underestimated. It is essential to focus not only on what actually happened, but on the potential.

KEY TERMS

Immediate cause

The unsafe act or unsafe condition that leads directly to the consequences (caused harm, damage, etc).

Root cause

An underlying circumstance that allowed the unsafe condition or act to exist (mainly organisational and management failings).

EXAMPLE

Piper Alpha

In the Piper Alpha disaster, the immediate cause was the release of flammable liquefied propane gas (LPG). The root causes of the release included failure of the permit-to-work system, inadequate lock-out and isolation standards, inadequate design standards, etc.

It may not be necessary to carry out a thorough investigation into all incidents; indeed, some have little potential for serious harm (eg minor cuts and bruises may receive a low level of investigation), but ignoring the true potential of an incident can be a costly mistake. Unless you fully understand your process (throughout its life cycle) and the interplay with things such as staffing levels and other organisational changes, it can be difficult to appreciate the potential risk.

We have already discussed the importance of learning from incidents. Investigations obviously help you do that. Ultimately, the purpose of the investigation is to prevent the accident from happening again as next time the outcome could be worse. There are, however, many other good reasons for investigating accidents and incidents.

Reasons for investigating accidents and incidents

These reasons are to:

- identify root causes and underlying causes of the incident;

- prevent the incident happening again (which could result in a more serious outcome next time);

- allow risk assessments to be updated so that organisations learn from past experience;

- document and record the details of the incident for future use;

- meet any legal requirements to report and investigate accidents and to assist with any civil claims that could result;

- enable patterns and trends to be discovered;

- demonstrate to staff and the public that there is a desire to improve and learn lessons, this will in turn improve morale in the organisation;

- determine if any disciplinary actions are needed. Though this can have an impact on morale it is sometimes necessary in serious cases.

It stands to reason that the benefits of accident investigation therefore flow from the reasons for investigation:

- once causes have been established, these can be addressed through revised risk assessments and the risk reduced;

- fewer serious events should occur as lower-level incidents are not allowed to escalate;

- legal compliance will be achieved;

- claims will be easier to deal with as the records and reports will be more readily available;

- workers will feel valued as even small incidents will result in action to keep them safe;

- any disciplinary action will be progressed fairly;

- by considering patterns and trends, hot spots or repeat issues can be addressed.

Plant workers discuss process trends.
©Crown Copyright, Health and Safety Executive

Organisational learning

3. Documented management processes to retain corporate knowledge

Earlier, we referred to the concept of 'corporate amnesia'. This is where organisations fail to retain their memory of previous incidents. Organisations are made up of individuals. If an organisation fails to actively record organisational learning (from past incidents), it will only retain that knowledge whilst specific individuals (those who can remember it) remain with the organisation. When they leave (career move or retirement, for example), the information and understanding is slowly lost until the organisation is in danger of repeating the same mistakes (or worse, reverses a critical intervention because the original reasons for doing it were lost). It is therefore essential for organisations to actively capture, record and disseminate critical information, data and reasoning on which decisions were based, as well as decisions themselves. In terms of documentation, this would typically include original design specifications and records of all subsequent plant modifications (we look at management of change later in this element).

4. Arrangements with other relevant organisations in sharing lessons learnt

Because major incidents are extremely rare, it is very limiting if organisations only look internally to learn lessons. A particular organisation may never have suffered a major incident, but there may be several examples out there of similar organisations, running similar processes, with similar control arrangements, who have had major incidents or near misses. If this information were shared, the potential benefits are much greater for the process industry as a whole. Process safety regulators and industry groups actively encourage information sharing in this way.

EXAMPLES

- In the UK, the Health and Safety Executive (HSE)[4] investigates and publishes reports on major accidents, emphasising the lessons to learn for related industries. They also publish specific safety alerts[5].

- The 'Responsible Care' programme has a global charter for members. One part of the programme is the voluntary sharing of information on best practice, risk management and the chemicals that are produced.

- The UK Institution of Chemical Engineers publishes a 'Loss Prevention Bulletin' that focuses on incidents and lessons for the wider industry.

- The Chemical Safety Board (CSB)[6] in the US carries out investigations into major incidents, including (but not confined to) those related to the process industries. Its results and findings are published and are often accompanied by videos and case studies to highlight deficiencies and where improvements can be made.

- In the oil and gas contracting sector, the International Association of Drilling Contractors[7] also publishes safety alerts. External information of this type, together with internal data on incidents, can therefore be used as 'lessons learnt' in the continual improvement process.

ACTIVITY

Visit the CSB's website at www.csb.gov and look at the information that is available to assist in process safety, including the videos that can be used for training. Read the news release into the findings of the Williams Olefins plant explosion and fire in Louisiana in 2013 as an example.

5. Purpose and use of benchmarking

Benchmarking is the process of comparing the performance of your own organisation against that of another, using standard, agreed criteria. This may mean reporting agreed data on a variety of performance indicators (such as number of unintentional releases/loss of containment events) in a given period or number of hours worked. When ranked against similar data reported by others in the industry, this helps you decide whether your performance is normal for the industry or significantly better (or worse) than average. This can drive change through the desire to improve.

Benchmarking can also yield benefits when seeking to implement or improve upon procedures. Many organisations are happy to share documentation such as management of change, permit-to-work and behavioural observation programme information if it can assist a fellow organisation.

6. Sources of Process Safety Management Information

Process safety management information is necessary for the safe operation and maintenance of process plant and should be documented, reliable, current and easily available to the people who need to use it.

Information internal to the organisation that will be needed to operate the plant within its safe operating envelope and to enable potential changes to be properly reviewed for their impact on safety and reliability could be:

- safety data sheets (SDS);

- process design criteria;

- process flow diagrams (PFD);

- safe operating procedures (SOPs) setting safe limits, such as for temperatures, pressures, flows, compositions and levels as well as evaluation of the effects;

- inspection, audit and investigation reports;

- maintenance records;

- piping and Instrument Diagrams (P&IDs);

- process control systems, including software integrity;

- relief system designs;

- fire detection and protection plans.

External information is available through the manufacturers' data, national legislation, any applicable European Union Directives (see: https://europa.eu/european-union/documents-publications_en), the UK Health and Safety Executive (see: www.hse.gov.uk), the US Occupational Safety and Health Administration (OSHA), trade associations and professional bodies such as the Institution of Chemical Engineers; International, European and British Standards; the International Labour Organisation (ILO) and other documents, all of which are often freely available on the Internet.

ACTIVITY

Take a look at the sources of information available in your organisation to assist in process safety management. Are they documented, reliable, current and easily available to the people who need to use them?

Visit the excellent HSE website at: www.hse.gov.uk/offshore/index.htm

---

Wylfa Nuclear Power Station.
©*Crown Copyright, Health and Safety Executive*

Management of change

1. Management of change control measures

The Flixborough disaster in the UK in 1974 highlighted the need for effective management of change processes all too well. Modifications to pipework to allow maintenance on a leaking vessel were carried out without proper consideration of the design requirements and by people without the required competence. The result was a pipe line that was not rated to withstand the pressures that it experienced and it ruptured, resulting in a release and explosion that killed 28 people. In the report[10] into the official inquiry, the following observation was made:

"No calculations were done to ascertain whether the bellows or pipe would withstand these strains; no reference was made to the relevant British Standard or any other accepted standard; no reference was made to the designer's guide issued by the manufacturers of the bellows; no drawing of the pipe was made, other than in chalk on the workshop floor; no pressure testing either of the pipe or the complete assembly was made before it was fitted. As a result, the assembly as constructed was of completely unknown strength and failed to comply with the British Standard..."[8]

Nypro Chemicals, Flixborough, fire and explosion incident.
©Crown Copyright, Health and Safety Executive

In the text *Chemical Process Safety: Learning from case histories*[9] such changes are described as "modifications made with good intentions" and there are many examples of where, despite trying to do the right thing for the plant, without the correct level of hazard evaluation, risk assessment and planning, the outcome was undesirable. These include tanks collapsing, road tankers failing and reactors exploding - at no point did the management intend to do the wrong thing, nevertheless the outcome was disastrous.

Formal documented system

An effective management of change (MOC) process is a cornerstone of process safety. It is a formally documented system developed to identify required modifications.

Requirement for hazard and risk analysis

The MOC process requires hazard identification and risk assessment to ensure that the full implications of any change are understood before it is put into practice, to ensure that new hazards are not introduced and that existing risks are not unwittingly increased. It should include procedures for both permanent and temporary modifications, and will include hardware and software changes. In order to capture all of the proposed changes, the process must be robustly implemented and this is often achieved by ensuring that a senior manager champions the process within the organisation, ensuring it is seen as an enabler rather than a barrier to engineering changes and removing any negative attitudes.

The MOC process should review the proposed modification to the existing operating parameters and design criteria. As well as the installation of new plant and equipment, the MOC process should be used to evaluate and record any planned changes to safety critical devices, replacement of equipment with non-identical alternatives, changes to alarms or other operating parameters, especially those that are outside the 'safe operating envelope' (this will be covered in more detail in Element 3). In some circumstances, changes to key workers (eg changing staffing levels) should be considered as requiring MOC.

This means that the following documentation may be required to support the MOC application:

- original process design criteria;

- existing process drawings;

- detail of proposed changes, including mechanical and electrical equipment specifications;

- details of trip and alarms planned;

- risk assessments or HAZOPS.

Process for all changes to be authorised

The MOC application must be:

- clearly defined and communicated to those in the approval process;

- submitted in advance of the change by the person proposing the modification to all relevant stakeholders (eg engineering, health and safety, production department, research and development, operational staff, maintenance workers, etc);

- tracked and managed as different stakeholders review and approve or make comments;

- given final approval by a suitably responsible person(s). Formal approval should be granted by senior management for the most significant changes (such as removal of safety critical devices).

Changes documented

All changes to process plant and process design should be correctly documented in order to ensure process knowledge retention:

- the MOC file should clearly document all of the changes proposed and be retained as a formal record;

- any process documents, eg process and instrumentation diagrams, operations manuals, etc should be updated with relevant changes;

- the MOC file should be retained with the design specifications for future reference.

Consult and inform

When consulting and informing those affected by the changes, the following needs to be considered:

- effective change management should be the result of collective decision-making and effective consultation rather than the decision of one individual;

- those affected should be consulted through the process and any changes should be communicated to those affected, including operational staff and maintenance workers.

Training

All staff should be trained in the need for MOC, the circumstances when MOC is necessary and the process for gaining MOC approval. Those in the approval process should receive additional training to ensure their competence.

THOUGHT PROVOKER

Think about your MOC process - either, one you are currently working with, or from a previous role. How effective is it? Is it valued by all involved? Is it rigorously used at all times? Could you make any improvements?

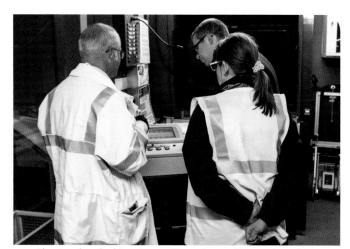

Plant workers looking at operating systems within nuclear plant.
©*Crown Copyright, Health and Safety Executive*

Worker engagement

Sometimes, legislation requires employers to consult with their workforce; even when this is not the case, it is still good practice to do so, and this can be achieved through either direct discussions with the workers or through worker representatives. This is because the workers have often experienced situations that give rise to concern or have ideas for improvements that could be made. They also provide valuable practical insight into the operation of the process that can greatly assist with the evaluation of proposed changes. Process industries make very extensive use of contractors, so they should also be involved in consultation, to reap the benefits and avoid the limitations. Consultation will necessarily be on a wide variety of subjects including process hazards, process controls, development of policies and process safety performance.

1. Benefits and limitations

Benefits from consultation are:

- better employer relationship with workers and contractors;

- clear demonstration of management commitment to process safety;

- closer co-operation that improves the safety culture;

- workers feeling more involved and more likely to be co-operative, and procedures more likely to be adhered to;

- practical insight into the operation or process and its hazards and operability/maintainability.

Limitations arising from consultation include:

- not all matters being agreed by true consultation - some decisions (such as staffing) may need to be taken at high level and imposed, and this can result in frustration;

- consultation takes time and this may not always be possible in the case where rapid decision-making is needed;

- some poorly structured consultation processes (eg poorly managed committees) may be disruptive rather than consultative, discussing trivia or non-safety matters rather than addressing core process safety issues.

KEY TERM

Consultation

The two-way exchange of information between parties, in this case between employer and worker. This is far more effective than the one-way exchange that we see when people are simply 'informed'.

An employer does not have to consult with workers on all matters, but there are some circumstances when it is advisable to do so; these include the:

- introduction of new measures that affect health and safety; these can include new process hazards and new or revised process controls;

- planning and implementation of new technologies that could affect health and safety;

- appointment of persons to provide health and safety advice or to assist in the development of emergency procedures;

- development of health and safety training;

- review of health and safety performance and the provision of health and safety information to the workforce;

- lessons learnt from incidents and near misses.

In addition, by engaging with workers, the employer can gain commitment and buy in when developing and implementing new policies.

2. Types of consultees and their role/responsibilities

There are several different methods of consulting with workers; these include:

- **Safety committees** - a formally established group of worker representatives who meet with management in order to assist in the two-way communication of information. The representatives are responsible for ensuring that the views of the groups that they represent are heard.

- **Discussion groups** - these are groups that are established to discuss issues of mutual interest, which can be work-related or not. These are often made up of volunteers with an interest in the topic.

- **Safety circles** - outside the formal discussions that workers may have with their representatives, workers may meet more informally to discuss safety problems in their workplace. This is an ideas-sharing group and any issues that require action are highlighted to the safety committee via the representatives for action.

- **Departmental meetings** - including health and safety at team and departmental meetings can provide a good opportunity for workers to voice concerns. These could then be passed to representatives or to management for action.

- **Email and web-based forums** - electronic communication media, such as multi-media messaging groups and online forums, can enable workers who may be remote from a central base to highlight and voice concerns. These methods will need to be overseen to ensure that the topics are appropriate and that appropriate issues are taken to the relevant team for action.

ACTIVITY

Write down all of the ways in which your organisation consults with workers. Which are truly consultative and which are informative? Can this be altered to increase consultation?

3. Necessity of including workers

Experience has shown that consultation that truly engages with workers yields huge benefits; for instance, when workers are involved in risk assessments, organisations gain a more accurate picture of the way the tasks are carried out, and benefit from practical suggestions for improvements and control measures. When workers are then involved in the development of procedures and safe systems of work, the implementation is less likely to be met with resistance from staff. In addition, workers' representatives can be invaluable during accident investigations and workplace inspections.

4. Engagement with workers should be a priority

As engagement is so important, it should be given high priority. For example, scheduling in committee meetings for the full year, and then sticking to the dates, provides a clear demonstration by management that they are committed to the process. Management should participate in the consultation process and not cancel meetings or fail to attend as that undermines the importance of the process. Plant stand downs or 'town hall' meetings can also be a useful demonstration of their commitment to engage with the workers. As a critical safety process, the arrangements for consulting and engaging should be audited like any other element of the safety management system. The audit could include:

- measurement of the number of the scheduled meetings that were held against the plan;

- the attendance at the meeting and the number of departments represented;

- the accuracy of the minutes and the rate of completion of any actions arising;

- the effectiveness of communication and extent to which they reached workers.

The findings should be reported to senior management as part of the audit of the safety management system.

Discussion between HSE inspector and plant operator.
©*Crown Copyright, Health and Safety Executive*

Competence

In this next section, we will explore the subject of competence. We have discussed the need for this many times already in different contexts. It is a core requirement for leaders (understanding the process and implications of decisions) when learning lessons, properly assessing and properly managing change.

1. The meaning of competence

KEY TERM

Competence

The ability to undertake responsibilities and to perform activities to a recognised standard on a regular basis... a combination of practical and thinking skills, experience and knowledge. (Source: HSE[10].)

There are legal requirements for employers to employ 'competent staff' - but what is competence? Competence has been defined over the years in many ways but, simply put, it is the blend of knowledge, skills and experience that enables a person to perform tasks well. It is more than completion of a course or obtaining a certificate, but a process that also requires the person to obtain practical experience to support his/her training.

2. The role of competence in safe working and behaviours

In health and safety terms, workers should be provided with training so that they know how to perform their job safely, from the day-to-day operational tasks in the production area, through to emergency procedures and specialist training for safety representatives, first aiders or emergency team members.

Training and competence ensures that workers have the relevant skills, knowledge and experience to carry out tasks that are required by their role. From the day-to-day operational tasks within the plant to the emergency response, permit-to-work and isolation procedures that are so important in process safety. Without adequate training, the decision as to what is the 'safe way' or the 'best way' to do a job would be left to the discretion of the individuals and this would result in wide and varied working standards. When the standards are clear, it is also easier for supervisors to monitor worker behaviour to ensure that compliance is maintained.

By training and ensuring the workers are competent, the employer can expect that a high level of compliance with safe working practices will be achieved, and that worker behaviours will be excellent.

Benefits of training include:

- new workers or those moving into a role can understand the requirements of the job much faster and are therefore safer;

- training to the correct standards will also ensure that the correct method of work is passed on rather than bad habits and unsafe actions;

- when tasks are performed to the right standard, fewer mistakes are made and productivity is generally higher. Well trained workers also feel valued and a solid training programme can assist in career development.

THOUGHT PROVOKER

Training is an essential part of building competency. When and how do you carry out safety training? Do you hold refresher training in safety topics? Are new workers more up to date with standards and requirements (after their safety induction) than longer-term workers?

3. Competency management systems

Not all workers need skills in all areas. While many requirements will be common to all workers, eg action to be taken on hearing an emergency alarm, many will depend on the role that people fulfil. For example, production operators will require training in permit-to-work, office-based staff may not, and some require specialist skills such as fire-fighting or first-aid training. Obviously, some workers will be specifically recruited for their technical expertise (such as chemical engineers) but will still need site and process-specific training. Key to this is defining the process safety-critical tasks that need to be carried out (routine, non-routine and emergency). Techniques such as task analysis will help here, as the tasks are looked at in detail (including potential for human error) and the skill-sets required for each step determined.

Different skill-set requirements (including the level and standard) can be rolled up into defined roles. Many organisations develop a training matrix as a starting point for developing individual competence and to provide a framework for career progression.

Example of a training matrix extract:

Role	Basic induction	Permit-to-work	Lock-out and isolation	Risk assessment	Management of change	Fire extinguisher
Production operator	✓	✓	✓	✓		✓
Shift fitter	✓	✓	✓	✓	✓	✓
Quality technician	✓			✓		
Process engineer	✓		✓	✓	✓	
Admin assistant	✓			✓		

The European Process Safety Centre[11] guidance suggests the following framework for competence management systems for process safety:

1. High-level policy statement, just like any other priority, it needs commitment from the top.

2. Facility minimum process safety competence (PSC) requirements. This is where the minimum-facility PSC requirements are identified and defined. For example, you might always need someone on hand with deep understanding of exothermic reactions and control of thermal runaways. Other requirements might depend on the life-cycle of the plant (design and build, commissioning vs normal use, for example).

3. Selection and recruitment of workers - a process for recruiting people with the right skills.

4. Individual competence needs analysis and managing competence gaps. This is making the general site requirements very specific for the needs of the task/role needed to be carried out. People are measured against these requirements and competence gaps identified.

5. Maintaining competence, training and development. The above gaps are filled with relevant training and other interventions. Refresher training will help maintain this.

6. Competence assessment and re-assessment. Training is all very well, but the ability to carry out the required critical function needs to be assessed and periodically re-assessed.

7. Special competence requirements for emergency situations. Emergencies (abnormal situations) subject people to much greater pressure than routine operation, so demands special training, eg to cope with the psychological stress and having to rapidly diagnose and act to bring a process back under control.

8. Ownership and commitment. Individuals need to be encouraged to be fully engaged in the need for, and development of, competence.

9. Continuous improvement. The effectiveness of the PSC management system itself needs to be periodically reviewed (competence requirements change over the life of a site, for example).

THOUGHT PROVOKER

How do you check competency after training? Attending a training session is one part of the jigsaw, but how does the organisation ensure that after training workers are truly competent?

Competence

4. Training and development programmes applicable to process safety risk

Some process safety risks are widely applicable across the sector and, indeed, there are general training courses aimed at different levels within the process industry. These tend to fall into three groups, aimed at:

- process safety leaders (senior executives and directors) - giving an overview of their responsibilities;

- managers, supervisors, designers, safety personnel and newly qualified engineers, giving fundamentals of PSM;

- operators and technicians - giving a detailed understanding of specific process hazards and controls that they are likely to encounter on site.

However, it is important not to limit the training to standard operating conditions, training may also be needed in non-standard operations (such as those covered in management of change processes) and also emergency situations (where safe shut-down is critical), and these may also include practical exercises.

It is essential to train process technicians on specific site hazards and controls.
©*Crown Copyright, Health and Safety Executive*

Element 1 **Process safety leadership**

Practice questions and references

References

1. Energy Institute, Process Safety (www.energyinst.org/technical/safety/process-safety)

2. HSE: Safety and environmental standards for fuel storage sites - Process Safety Leadership Group - Final Report

3. Corporate Governance for Process Safety: Guidance for Senior Leaders in High Hazard Industries (www1.oecd.org/officialdocuments/publicdisplaydocumentpdf/?cote=ENV/JM/MONO(2012)39&docLanguage=En)

4. HSE (www.hse.gov.uk/comah/accidents.htm)

5. HSE (www.hse.gov.uk/safetybulletins)

6. Chemical Safety Board (www.csb.gov)

7. International Association of Drilling Contractors (www.iadc.org/safety-alerts)

8. The Flixborough disaster, Report of the court of inquiry (www.icheme.org/communities/special-interest-groups/safety%20and%20loss%20prevention/resources/~/media/Documents/Subject%20Groups/Safety_Loss_Prevention/HSE%20Accident%20Reports/The%20Flixborough%20Disaster%20-%20Report%20of%20the%20Court%20of%20Inquiry.pdf)

9. Sanders, R. Chemical process safety, learning from case histories

10. COMAH Competent Authority, Inspection of Competence Management Systems at COMAH Establishments, Operational Delivery Guide, produced by the HSE, EA, SEPA. http://www.hse.gov.uk/comah/guidance/inspection-competence-management-systems.pdf

11. EPSC, Making the Case for Process Safety Competence (www.epsc.org/data/files/Process%20Safety%20Competence/Making%20the%20Case%20for%20Process%20Safety%20Competence.pdf)

Practice questions

Q1. Process safety mainly deals with:

A   high frequency, high severity risks.

B   low frequency, high severity risks.

C   low frequency, low severity risks.

D   high frequency, low severity risks.

Q2. Within a management of change procedure, final approval for removal of a safety critical device should be given by a:

A   senior manager.

B   lead operator.

C   chemical engineer.

D   process technician.

Q3. Benchmarking is used to identify good practice across similar:

A   committees.

B   organisations.

C   techniques.

D   procedures.

Q4. What is the most important benefit of involving workers when carrying out risk assessments?

A   To reduce resistance and conflict when risk assessments are introduced.

B   To make sure there is a balanced representation of workers and managers.

C   To enable employer and employees to comply fully with legal requirements.

D   To gather detailed practical knowledge about workplace hazards and risks.

Q5. Which of the following is the most direct evidence of worker competence?

A   Consistently performing a work-related task correctly to the required standard.

B   Signing a document to confirm that a procedure was read and understood.

C   Completing an attendance form following a process safety toolbox talk.

D   Carrying out a work-related task without harming themselves or others.

Notes

ELEMENT 1

ELEMENT 2

ELEMENT 3

ELEMENT 4

Element 1 answers: Q1 - B; Q2 - A; Q3 - B; Q4 - D; Q5 - A

Management of process risk

Lifting operations within an oil refinery.
©Crown Copyright, Health and Safety Executive

This element will look at the elements of a process safety management system and at risk management techniques used in the industry. It will also explain what a permit-to-work is used for, and how to select and manage contractors.

Learning outcomes

On completion of this element, you should be able to:

2.1 Outline the purpose and importance of establishing a process safety management system and its key elements.

2.2 Outline common risk management techniques used in process industries.

2.3 Outline asset management and maintenance strategies for process plant.

2.4 Explain the role, purpose and features of a permit-to-work.

2.5 Explain the key principles of safe shift handover.

2.6 Explain the principles of selecting, assessing and managing contractors.

Establishing a process safety management system

1. Reasons for developing an integrated and comprehensive process safety management system

Good process safety management does not happen by accident. Management of health and safety in any type of organisation requires clearly defined processes, and process safety management is no different in that respect.

There are clear moral, legal and financial reasons for developing a process safety management system.

The **moral** reason for managing process safety is clear if we study recent disasters. Process safety failures result in fatalities in extreme circumstances. The Piper Alpha disaster in 1988 resulted in 167 deaths and the Transocean Deepwater Horizon explosion in a further 11 in 2010, these were all preventable and needless fatalities.

Effective process safety management will help an organisation meet **legal** obligations, as it will assist compliance with legislation and any internal corporate compliance standards.

The **financial** argument for managing process safety centres around the knowledge that the costs of failure are so catastrophic. If we look at, for example, the Deepwater Horizon disaster, that one incident alone resulted in 11 fatalities, almost 5 million barrels of oil polluted the sea and, as a result, each of the main players in the incident (Transocean, BP and Haliburton) received multibillion dollar fines, but the real costs came as a result of compensation payouts. With no upper cap in place, the total financial impact to BP alone is in the region of $62 billion.

2. Elements of a process safety management system

While in personal safety we might look to HSG65 or OHSAS 18001 for a framework, in process safety there are similar elements that can be viewed here alongside the safety management system (SMS) to aid comparisons. Some process safety management system (PSMS) elements will be unique due to the hazards; others simply contain a different level of emphasis. Opposite, you can see the comparison between the two:

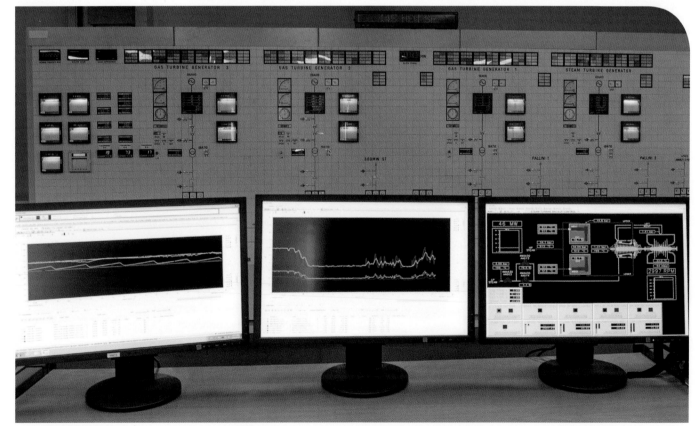

Monitors in a control room of a natural gas power plant.

Element 2 **Management of process risk**

PSMS Element	Comment	Where it fits in a typical SMS structure, eg OHSAS 18001
Strong Leadership	Good safety leadership is essential as this establishes priority, determines resource levels, and sets direction and the culture of the organisation. Their commitment to PSM will be echoed through the business.	Policy
Hazard Analysis	Hazard analysis is required of both the process and the equipment/plant. This will require not only the identification of hazards but also the evaluation of the potential outcomes for each scenario. Any residual risks need to be known and understood.	Planning (Hazard Identification and Risk Assessment/Control)
Management of Change	Management of change is a formal process to identify the potential consequences of changes before they are put into practice. This includes checks before the change is implemented and before start-up.	Planning (Risk Assessment/Control) and Implementation and Operation (Operational Control)
Operation within Design Intent	There needs to be a clearly defined set of procedures and safe systems of work that ensure that the plant and process are operated within their design parameters. This should cover normal operations, start-up and shut-down procedures, maintenance, cleaning and emergency situations.	Implementation and Operation (Documentation and Operational Control)
Competence Management	There is an emphasis on competence for obvious reasons. This includes the need for training both on introduction to a site or process, refresher training and when there are significant changes in the process.	Implementation and Operation (Competence)
Control of Contractors	Contractors are widely used within the process industries, therefore effective contractor control is essential.	Implementation and Operation (Operational Control, Communication, Participation, Consultation)
Asset Integrity	This ensures that critical equipment is fit for purpose (specification, quality), installed correctly and maintained. It combines planned preventive maintenance, condition monitoring and testing. The organisation will need to identify the critical equipment but this will typically include pressure relief and emergency shut-down devices, alarms and sensors, as well as pressure systems (process vessels, pipe lines, piping etc) whose failure could cause loss of containment of hazardous substances.	Planning (Risk Assessment/Control) Implementation and Operation (Operational Control)
Emergency Response	The emergency response will include on-site and off-site response to foreseeable incidents, such as evacuation, fire and rescue, first aid and mitigation of loss of containment.	Implementation and Operation (Emergency Preparedness)
Process Safety-Related Incident Recording and Investigation	Process safety-related incidents (and near misses) include the seemingly minor events that are often overlooked but could easily escalate if not investigated and controlled. These include faulty level sensors and minor excursions which, under other circumstances, could have had much more serious consequences. Just like other safety incidents, these process safety incidents should be investigated to continually improve the process.	Checking
Performance Monitoring and Auditing	Finally, there is a need for performance measurement. This uses leading and lagging process safety indicators to determine if the safety processes are operating correctly. Internal auditing is also needed to check performance of the PSMS elements.	Checking

Establishing a process safety management system

ACTIVITY

Review the systems you have in place for process safety management - how many of the elements from the table on page 25 do you have in place?

The use of a clearly documented PSMS containing the elements outlined on page 25 broadly follows the plan-do-check-act model.

Effective process safety management, like all effective safety management, is the product of a structured and focused effort that places health and safety at the centre of business decisions and not as an after-thought. There are many different models of safety management systems, but all follow the same plan-do-check-act cycle (known as 'PDCA') as part of a continual improvement process. In the PDCA cycle, the following broad steps are taken:

- plan - establish a clear set of goals and targets that will move the organisation forward in terms of health and safety management;

- do - carry out actions to improve health and safety;

- check - monitor and determine whether the steps you have taken are moving you closer to your goals. These measures can include accident investigation findings and will be explored more fully later in the element;

- act - take action as a result of the monitoring findings in order to continually improve the process.

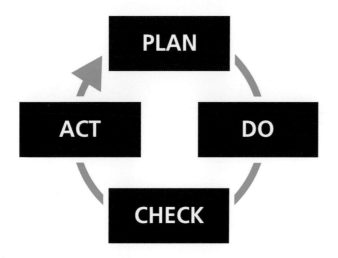

PDCA management cycle

In process safety management systems, the same basic structure is followed:

- policy (plan);

- planning (plan);

- implementation and operation (do);

- checking and corrective action (check;

- management review (act);

- continual improvement (act).

Health and safety management systems sections

Health and safety policy (plan)

This should be a clear demonstration of the aims of the organisation towards health and safety, together with the vision and commitment to achieve these goals. It should also commit to complying with legislation and to continually improving the processes. It should come from board level.

Health and safety planning (plan)

This should include the processes for the identification of hazards and the reduction of risks. The plan should then seek to deliver a reduction in risk while prioritising the biggest issues. At the same time, the plan should also identify potential breaches of, or changes in, legislation, and address these.

Implementation and operation (do)

This section contains the roles and responsibilities for those who will deliver the objectives in the health and safety plan, though senior management remain accountable for health and safety. Those given responsibilities need to be competent to deliver them.

This section also contains the risk control systems required to address the specific hazards and risks. It will include the design procedures for such systems (eg pressure relief, control, alarm, shut-down, safe operating procedures, maintenance arrangements, competency procedures, etc). Site safety procedures, including permit-to-work and emergency procedures, will also be included in this section, together with details of the processes in place to engage with the workers. All documents generated will need to be controlled.

Checking and corrective action (check)

In order to determine if progress is being made towards the goals, there should be monitoring and measurement activities carried out. These will include active and reactive measures (also known as 'leading' and 'lagging' indicators), the most widely used are accident investigations and statistics, but will not be very effective for process safety hazards because process safety accidents will be rare. Near misses will be a better lagging indicator and leading indicators (eg planned maintenance backlog) will be important as they can identify potential problems before an incident occurs. As well as monitoring against the targets, there should also be assessments to determine whether the legislation is being complied with. Finally, there should be internal audits to determine the overall effectiveness of the health and safety management system.

Management review (act)

Lastly, management should carry out regular reviews of the management system to review the data and ensure that the plan remains relevant to feed the continual improvement process. This should lead to action, as necessary, to correct issues with the PSMS.

> **THOUGHT PROVOKER**
>
> Think about your health and safety policy. Does everyone know what it says and what the organisation aims are with regard to health and safety - especially process safety?

3. Licence to operate

Some high-hazard processes, such as oil and gas and some chemical processes, require the operator to apply for a licence in order to operate, and this is a legally required process in some countries (licences are not the only legal means of controlling operations but are a very common means). In order to gain such a licence (or otherwise be able to commence or continue operation), the operator may have to produce a document known as a 'safety case', which demonstrates that:

- all hazards with the potential to result in a major accident have been identified;

- all major accident risks have been evaluated and robust controls are in place (or, for new processes, that they are being implemented) and that the operator can demonstrate compliance with any legal obligations;

- risks are controlled to as low as reasonably practicable (ALARP).

4. Purpose and typical content of a major accident prevention policy (MAPP)

The UK Control of Major Accident Hazards Regulations 2015 (COMAH) place numerous requirements on high-hazard installations operators. One such requirement is that operators produce a major accident prevention policy (MAPP). A MAPP contains:

- details of the organisational responsibilities for delivering safety at the site;

- identification of the major accident hazards (eg loss of containment, fire, toxic chemicals) and the means by which the risk is assessed;

- the operational control methods used to reduce and control the risks;

- the emergency plans (on site and off site) that are in place and the procedures to control emergency situations;

- the processes for monitoring and auditing of the process and the means by which the MAPP will be reviewed.

Accident investigators examine the causes of an industrial explosion.
©*Crown Copyright, Health and Safety Executive*

Establishing a process safety management system

5. Leading and lagging process safety performance indicators

In order to determine how well the site is managing process safety, there must be some checks and balances; this appears in the "checking and corrective action" section of the process safety management system, and is achieved by implementing process safety indicators (PSIs), which we started to explore in Element 1. PSIs are specific safety measures that can be implemented in the process sector. They must be relevant to the organisation and take into consideration the hazards and potentials that exist on the site. Time and time again, when major incidents occur, management will state that they have an "excellent safety record", yet the operators may have been aware of the risks. In these instances, what management mean is, "we haven't had a major injury for years" while the operators may be all too aware of the failing plant infrastructure that they see on a day-to-day basis. PSIs should ideally be chosen to reveal such weaknesses.

The HSE COMAH publication Process Safety Indicators[1] (operational delivery guide) states the following: *"There is a need for a robust and systematic process safety management system supported by strong process safety leadership from board level down throughout the organisation in order to achieve the right culture and enable key decision makers to understand all the dimensions of process safety risk when making business and operational decisions. Good management decisions can only be made on the basis of sound information and PSPIs provide the means to highlight key issues of process safety management performance."* (Process Safety Performance Indicators - COMAH.)

Effective PSIs will focus on meaningful actions to improve the safety of the site rather than minutiae like carrying drinks in lidded cups, after all, it is not worth worrying about a potential scald if there is a reasonable likelihood that the plant will explode! Good PSIs will enable the board to make meaningful and informed decisions about the site. The report into the Grangemouth refinery accident in the UK cited one problem, "Companies should develop key performance indicators for major hazards and ensure process safety performance is monitored and reported against these parameters".

PSIs can be divided into two types: leading indicators and lagging indicators.

This can be carried out by a combination of methods - the HSE publication *HSG254 Developing process safety indicators*[2] suggests one method is by combining leading indicators, lagging indicators and audits.

> **KEY TERMS**
>
> **Leading indicators**
>
> Proactive measurements of conditions that monitor process safety before something goes wrong and to see if things are operating as intended.
>
> **Lagging indicators**
>
> Reactive measures that look at failures, such as the number of injuries, the number of near misses and the number of spills which are reported, or excursions where plant is operated outside the intended operational envelope.

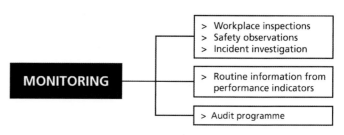

Health and Safety Monitoring Activities
Source: HSG254 Developing process safety indicators: A step-by-step guide for chemical and major hazard industries, HSE, 2006 (www.hse.gov. uk/pubns/priced/hsg254.pdf)

Leading indicators seek to find issues with the process safety management before incidents or injuries occur. They explore, for example, the number of toolbox talks delivered vs the plan, the percentage of safe behaviours observed or the testing of emergency procedures. Leading indicators are a good way of monitoring process safety as small deviations can be identified and addressed long before they result in harm.

Lagging indicators use incidents such as spillages and releases, accidents, injuries and other unwanted events as indicators of process safety failure to enable corrective actions to be developed. Lagging indicators are a valid monitoring tool, but they are limited as they do rely on something going wrong (they do not prevent the incident from occurring).

HSG254 also suggests that organisations should use leading and lagging indicators in combination in order to manage process safety risk:

- a team should be established to implement the monitoring process. This must have a champion at senior level;

- determine what can go wrong in the process and where;

- identify the risk controls that would prevent such an incident and establish a lagging indicator that would measure that failure;

- establish the critical actions for each risk control system and develop leading indicators for each that can be monitored to ensure the risk control systems work as intended;

- monitor and collect data and report on findings;

- review to ensure that the process is working.

The HSE in the UK has published "HSG254 Developing process safety indicators: A step-by-step guide for chemical and major hazard industries" and has listed examples of lagging and leading indicators for an inspection and maintenance risk control system, starting with the desired safety outcomes:

"Desired safety outcomes:

- no unexpected loss of containment due to failure of flexi hoses, couplings, pumps, valves, flanges, fixed pipes, bulk tanks or instrumentation;

- no unexpected loss of containment due to blockages in tank vents;

- no fires or explosions due to static electric ignition;

- no fires or explosions caused by a source of ignition from faulty or damaged hazardous area electrical equipment;

- fire detection and fire-fighting equipment is available and in good condition.

Potential lagging indicators:

- number of unexpected loss-of-containment incidents due to failure of flexi hoses, couplings, pumps, valves, flanges, fixed pipes, bulk tanks or instrumentation;

- number of loss-of-containments due to blockages in tank vents;

- number of fires or explosions that result from a static electric ignition;

- number of fires or explosions caused by a source of ignition from faulty or damaged hazardous area electrical equipment;

- number of incidents of fire/explosion where fire detection or fire-fighting equipment failed to function as designed.

Potential leading indicators:

- percentage of safety critical plant/equipment that performs within specification when inspected;

- percentage of safety critical plant and equipment inspections completed to schedule;

- percentage of maintenance actions identified that are completed to the specified timescale;

- percentage of fault trending carried out to schedule."

Percentage of safety critical plant inspections undertaken to schedule is one type of leading indicator.

Establishing a process safety management system

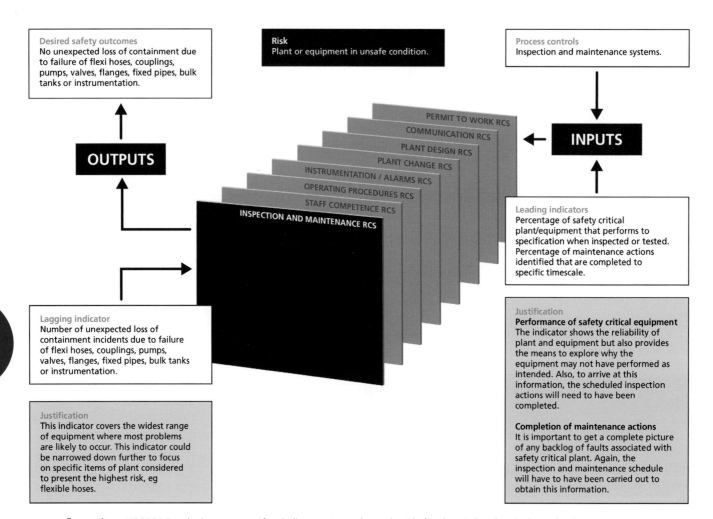

Desired safety outcomes
No unexpected loss of containment due to failure of flexi hoses, couplings, pumps, valves, flanges, fixed pipes, bulk tanks or instrumentation.

Risk
Plant or equipment in unsafe condition.

Process controls
Inspection and maintenance systems.

OUTPUTS

PERMIT TO WORK RCS
COMMUNICATION RCS
PLANT DESIGN RCS
PLANT CHANGE RCS
INSTRUMENTATION / ALARMS RCS
OPERATING PROCEDURES RCS
STAFF COMPETENCE RCS
INSPECTION AND MAINTENANCE RCS

INPUTS

Leading indicators
Percentage of safety critical plant/equipment that performs to specification when inspected or tested. Percentage of maintenance actions identified that are completed to specific timescale.

Lagging indicator
Number of unexpected loss of containment incidents due to failure of flexi hoses, couplings, pumps, valves, flanges, fixed pipes, bulk tanks or instrumentation.

Justification
Performance of safety critical equipment
The indicator shows the reliability of plant and equipment but also provides the means to explore why the equipment may not have performed as intended. Also, to arrive at this information, the scheduled inspection actions will need to have been completed.

Completion of maintenance actions
It is important to get a complete picture of any backlog of faults associated with safety critical plant. Again, the inspection and maintenance schedule will have to have been carried out to obtain this information.

Justification
This indicator covers the widest range of equipment where most problems are likely to occur. This indicator could be narrowed down further to focus on specific items of plant considered to present the highest risk, eg flexible hoses.

Source from: HSG254 Developing process safety indicators: A step-by-step guide for chemical and major hazard industries, HSE, 2006

ELEMENT 1

ELEMENT 2

ELEMENT 3

ELEMENT 4

The HSG254 guidance also suggests the following method for developing leading and lagging process safety indicators:

Table 1 Overview of the six steps to setting performance indicators		
Step 1	Establish the organisational arrangements to implement the indicators	Appoint a steward or champion
		Set up an implementation team
		Senior management should be involved
Step 2	Decide on the scope of the measurement system. Consider what can go wrong and where	Select the organisational level
		Identify the scope of the measurement system: • identify incident scenarios - what can go wrong?; • identify the immediate causes of hazard scenarios; • review performance and non-conformances.
Step 3	Identify the risk control systems in place to prevent major accidents. Decide on the outcomes for each and **set a lagging indicator**	What risk control systems are in place?
		Describe the outcome
		Set a lagging indicator
		Follow up deviations from the outcome
Step 4	Identify the critical elements of each risk control system, (ie those actions or processes that must function correctly to deliver the outcomes) and **set leading indicators**	What are the most important parts of the risk control system?
		Set leading indicators
		Set tolerances
		Follow up deviations from tolerances
Step 5	Establish the data collection and reporting system	Collect information - ensure information/ unit of measurement is available or can be established
		Decide on presentation format
Step 6	Review	Review performance of process management system
		Review the scope of the indicators
		Review the tolerances

Adapted from HSG254 Developing process safety indicators: A step-by-step guide for chemical and major hazard industries, HSE, 2006

Establishing a process safety management system

6. Auditing compliance and identifying improvement opportunities

Auditing is the final step in the review process and a tool to drive for continual improvements in process safety. There are many different types of audit, from process safety through to quality and compliance auditing, but they all share similar characteristics.

KEY TERMS

Auditing

This can be defined as the *"systematic, objective critical evaluation of how well an organisation's management system is performing by examining evidence".*

Health and safety audits, like any other audit, are a process used to determine compliance with a standard. This could be an external standard that allows accreditation (such as OHSAS 18001) or an internal health and safety management system. It seeks to determine if there are appropriate management systems in place to manage health and safety, and that suitable risk control systems and workplace precautions are implemented and working.

Audits are part of the continual improvement process and therefore should be seen as a proactive measure to improve performance, not as a negative review looking for failures. Some audits are necessary and are required by certification bodies; others are implemented as a best-practice approach to improve safety overall, but in either case the intent is the same: to identify areas for improvement that can then feed new health and safety plans.

An auditor provides feedback to a senior manager.
©Crown Copyright, Health and Safety Executive

Risk management techniques used within the process industries

Managing process risk is clearly one of the main objectives of a process safety management system. This section will look at the range of techniques available.

1. Purpose and use of risk assessment

Risk assessments are essential in the management of safety in all workplaces - simply put, it is a process that identifies hazards, evaluates risks by considering the likelihood of harm occurring and the potential severity of the event that could result. Risk controls are then identified, which reduce the risk to an acceptable level.

> **KEY TERMS**
>
> **Hazard**
>
> Something that has the potential to cause harm.
>
> **Risk**
>
> This is the likelihood that a hazard will cause harm, in a combination with the severity of injury, damage or loss that might foreseeably occur.

There are no prescribed formats for risk assessments - the UK's HSE has a simple five-step approach that is effective for many simpler operations:

Step 1: Identify the hazards

▼

Step 2: Identify the people who might be harmed and how

▼

Step 3: Evaluate the risk and decide on precautions

▼

Step 4: Record the significant findings

▼

Step 5: Review and update as necessary

Adapted from INDG163: Five steps to risk assessment[2]

This process works well for less complex operations, but there are occasions where more advanced risk assessment techniques are needed and, here, the greater effort is justified by the higher level of risks involved. As previously explored in Element 1, there are sometimes regulatory requirements for safety cases that contain highly detailed risk assessments that are far above the level achieved by the five-step approach. The HSE therefore recommends the following approach in their publication Offshore Information Sheet 3/2006 - *Guidance on Risk Assessment for Offshore Installations*[3].

Risk management techniques used within the process industries

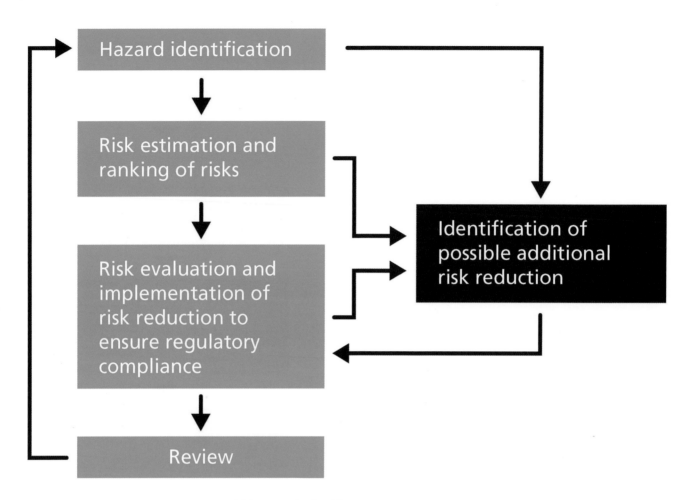

Main stages in the risk assessment process
Adapted from: Offshore Information Sheet 3/2006 - Guidance on Risk Assessment for Offshore Installations

THOUGHT PROVOKER

What are the biggest risks faced by your organisation? How well are these risks being controlled? Can you think of any obvious risk-reduction measures that are needed? If so, how can you bring this to management's attention?

2. Qualitative, quantitative and semi-quantitative risk assessments

The risk assessment process can use a variety of methods to assess the level of risks, and have been adapted from the HSE's Offshore Installation Sheet 3/2006:

- qualitative (Q), in which frequency and severity are determined purely qualitatively, eg low, medium, high;

- semi-quantitative (SQ), in which frequency and severity are approximately quantified within ranges;

- quantified risk assessment (QRA), in which full quantification occurs by the use of known data.

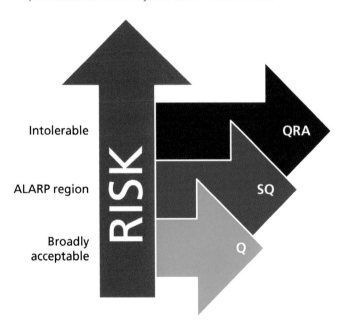

Proportionate risk assessment
Source from Offshore Installation Sheet 3/2006 - Guidance on Risk Assessment for Offshore Installations

As the risk increases, so does the need for more rigorous risk assessment and consideration/implementation of more robust controls (this is the principle of proportionality). In the process industry, this means that fully quantified risk assessment is rarely needed; often, semi-quantitative is sufficient, eg where safety cases are required. However, in some cases, fully quantified risk assessment may be required. Indeed, this is sometimes a regulatory requirement.

3. Barrier models

The barrier modelling concept considers that actions or 'barriers' can be used to prevent hazards from resulting in losses, which could be anything from a fatality to a loss of containment or environmental release. If the process relies on one barrier, such as a high-level alarm, then if this fails, there is no other means of protection. If there are multiple barriers in place, as in the Swiss cheese model, then there will only be a failure if the defect occurs in each layer and these are all aligned at the same time (ie the holes in the Swiss cheese line up).

> **ACTIVITY**
>
> Research the Swiss cheese model using search engines to ensure that you have a good understanding of the concept.

4. The application of risk management tools to identify and assess process safety risk

There are a number of different tools that can be used, and these are most effective if the management of risk is initially considered at the concept and design stage, where changes can be made relatively easily. Before start-up, a more complete assessment of risk should be carried out to ensure that nothing has changed and that the process will operate as intended. Additional controls may need to be implemented during unusual process activities, such as start-up and shut-down.

Risk management techniques used within the process industries

5. Hazard realisation

Some risk assessment models use the concept of 'hazard realisation' and 'barriers' rather than the more simplistic hazards, risks and control measures we have seen already. In risk realisation, the assessor asks "what if" and then explores the issue further to look at the true potential of an incident (we will look at this in more detail later).

Hazard realisation requires the assessor to act as a 'prophet of doom' and look at worst-case scenarios, but for good reason. If these potentials are understood, the controls can be implemented in the form of 'barriers', which we will explore in a moment.

So, for the loss of containment of flammable liquid for example, the assessment could be as follows:

- **What:**

  - loss of containment of acetone.

- **Where:**

  - from delivery pump, supply lines, recirculating pump, flexible delivery hoses or tank.

- **When:**

  - at a time when the area is occupied (weekday) or,

  - at a weekend when plant is less occupied and it may be undetected.

- **How:**

  - poorly maintained pump;

  - gasket failure;

  - leaking fittings or instrumentation;

  - split hoses;

  - overfilled tanks or vessels;

  - poor offloading connection.

- **Why:**

  - inadequate planned maintenance;

  - introduction of ignition source (electrical equipment that is incorrect or poorly maintained, smoking, hot work, human error, static, arson);

  - no detection for release apart from human observations;

  - plant not fully staffed at weekends.

- **Potential outcome:**

  - spillage, fire, explosion, loss of plant and loss of workers.

Bow tie model

As you work through the hazard realisation then 'barriers' can be identified that can be placed between the initiator (the triggering event) to either prevent it from happening or to mitigate the outcome. These can be termed, 'lines of defence' (LOD) or 'layers of protection' (LOP) and are exactly that – actions which, if implemented, could prevent the initiating event from resulting in a release or harm, or mitigating the consequences should it occur. If these are drawn together, this is known as a 'bow tie' diagram, due to its shape. When drawn, each of the barriers can be labelled with a reference number to make recording of the barriers easier. An example of a bow tie diagram is shown next.

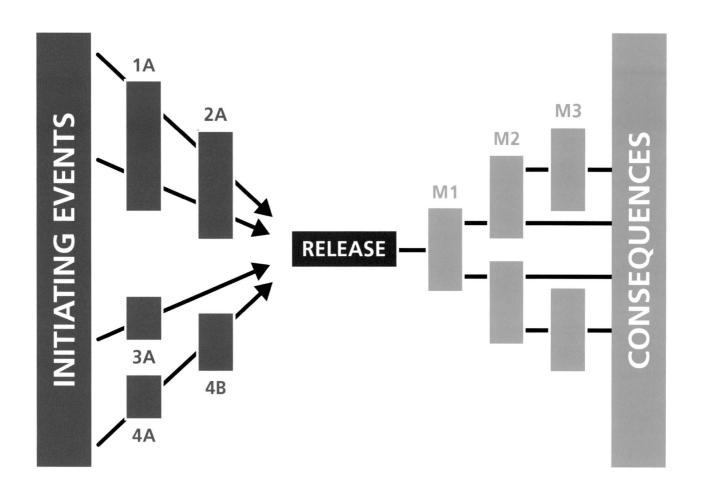

EXAMPLE BARRIERS

> Plant layout
> Construction standards
> Inspection
> Instrumentation

EXAMPLE BARRIERS

> Detection system
> ESD (emergency shut down)
> Active protection
> Passive protection
> EER (escape, evacuation and rescue)

Based on offshore information sheet No. 3/2006 Guidance on risk assessment for offshore installations, HSE, 2006 (www.hse.gov.uk/offshore/sheet32006.pdf)

In the previous example, the barriers to prevent the release may include:

- plant specification standards;

- maintenance standards;

- high level and high-high level alarms on vessels.

Mitigation to reduce the consequences may include:

- layout to locate flammable storage away from heavily occupied areas;

- bunds and containment;

- electrical equipment specified for flammable areas;

- fire walls/blast walls;

- isolation valves in drains.

Risk management techniques used within the process industries

Hazard and operability study (HAZOP)

A Hazard and Operability study (HAZOP) is an advanced risk assessment first used by ICI in the 1960s. It is a very thorough analysis of a process to identify ways in which the process could deviate from its design intention, in order that controls can be developed. It is usually chaired by an independent HAZOP leader and involves a multidisciplinary team of designers, engineers, safety professionals, operators in the area and other specialists.

The HAZOP is a 'bottom-up' technique, which uses prompts about what could cause the process to lose control, or to deviate from the design intent. A HAZOP is carried out on piping and instrumentation diagrams (P&ID) and breaks the process down into small sections, known as 'nodes', and for each node identifies a parameter to be examined, eg flow. A series of guidewords (such as 'no', 'less', 'more') are agreed upfront and combined with each parameter to form a 'deviation'. For the parameter 'flow' you would have deviations 'no flow', 'less flow', 'more flow', etc. The team then determines potential causes or reasons for the deviation and, in turn, put controls in place to prevent that from occurring; this could range from design changes to increased maintenance.

The HAZOP findings are recorded in a tabular format and retained as evidence of the study.

See below an extract from a HAZOP of a domestic shower:

THOUGHT PROVOKER

Who would usefully be included in a HAZOP team in your organisation? Have you been involved? Would you have the in-house skills to manage the HAZOP process or would you need independent help?

Parameter	Guideword	Deviation	Cause	Consequence	Action
Temperature	More	More temperature	More flow hot water	Scald	Install thermostatic valve
			Boiler too high	Scald	Maintenance, trained operators
			Less flow cold - other taps used	Scald	Investigate engineering solution
Temperature	Less	Less temperature	More flow cold	Discomfort	Thermostatic valve will address
			Boiler too low	Discomfort	Maintenance, trained operators
			Less flow hot - other taps used	Discomfort	No further action needed as not safety critical

ELEMENT 1

ELEMENT 2

ELEMENT 3

ELEMENT 4

Hazard Identification (HAZID)

A hazard identification (HAZID) study is a structured, team-based approach to identify hazards, their potential consequences, and requirements for risk reduction before changes are made to existing processes and plant. This is sometimes carried out in a walk-through, but can be carried out at a desk using software. A HAZID study considers the process safety hazards as well as the non-process hazards such as transport and manual handling. These hazards are then used to feed the risk assessment process.

HAZID is a top-down study which is structured by keywords, based on the type of hazards you want to avoid, eg toxic release, overtemperature, overpressure, fire, explosion, etc, applied to a whole flowsheet at a time, to work out if and how that hazard could be realised in the process you are studying. While HAZOP is cause-driven, HAZID is consequence-driven.

In the same way, as with HAZOP, team members should be typically three to six, plus a facilitator and scribe. The construction of the team may change, but essentially there should be a core of facilitator, scribe, facilities or operations engineer and safety engineer. In the case of older installations, it would be beneficial to have at least one senior operator who knows the process well and how it operates. These would be supported by structural, construction, electrical, machinery, and process design as appropriate.

Drawings often used in a HAZID study are escape route drawings, process flow diagrams and P&ID that give the location of emergency shut-down valves, relief or blow down valves, deluge valves and fire extinguishers.

HAZID is designed to identify the mechanisms by which safety objectives may be violated. These may be hardware, such as mechanical failure, or software, such as management systems or procedures. For example, a safety objective could be the containment of fluids and a violation could be caused by impact, corrosion or fatigue. See the worked example below.

After the sessions, it will be necessary to quantify the various events as to their consequence and frequency. The final values must then be ranked against pre-determined criteria and prioritised.

The final list of events or hazards can then become the core of the safety case and a set of integrated and objective safety studies set in motion.

Failure Mode Effect Analysis (FMEA)

A Failure Mode Effect Analysis (FMEA) is a study often used to brainstorm how a component or system might fail, the potential effects/consequences of those failures, existing safeguards against those failure modes and whether more should be in place. Again, it is a brainstorming type of activity often documented in a tabular format. The FMEA requires the multidisciplinary team to identify for each component of the system:

- failure modes - ways in which the system can fail;

- effect - what will happen as a result of the failure;

- severity - how severe the impact is to the user/customer;

- cause - possible causes of the failure mode;

- occurrence - how often is this likely to happen;

- detection mode - what controls are currently in place to spot the defect before it happens, or detect it if it occurs;

- detection - the probability that the failure will reach the user without being detected;

- Risk Priority Number (RPN) - severity × occurrence × detection = RPN;

- recommended actions - what action is recommended, by whom and by when;

Guide Word	Event Nature	Cause Violation	Consequence Escalation	Control of Mitigating Factors	Hazard Index Cons. × Freq.		Action Required Comments
Failure of pressure vessel	Leaking flange	Gasket failure	Loss of containment	Likely to be progressive if corrosion	H	L	Review the reliability of fitted gaskets
Failure of flange weld	Leaking oil line	Corrosion or impact	Catastrophic failure leading to large HCL	Six-monthly NDT PIG conducted	H	L	Review welding protocols and post welding NDT

Risk management techniques used within the process industries

- RPNs - used to prioritise actions;

- actions taken - what action was actually carried out.

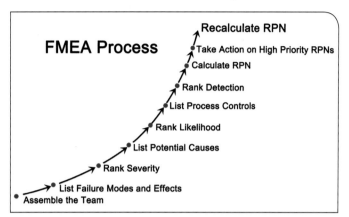

Failure mode and effects analysis (FMEA) process.

When determining the severity, occurrence or detection, the assessors agree a set of criteria that are used throughout the assessments to ensure that, for each failure mode, the same criteria are applied. For example, for severity the scale could be as follows:

1. Minor incident, no injury or pollution.

2. Minor injury, small spill.

3. Loss of containment, major injury.

4. Major incident, such as fire or pollution event with very high potential.

5. Fatality.

Event tree analysis (ETA)

Event trees are used to evaluate the mitigation measures that will operate after an event. The process starts with the initiating event (the 'disaster') and works forward in time to see what protective measures will operate. Each control will either be a 'success' or a 'failure' and, in this way, branches are built up on the tree. The branch for the initiating event of a fire is shown below - it will either be detected or it won't.

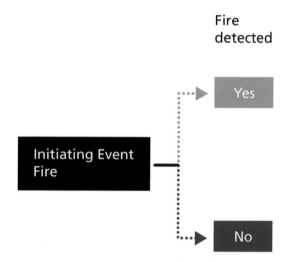

We then continue the branch along; if the fire is detected, the next step is for the alarm to sound. It may sound or may not, and this adds another branch to the tree. However, if the fire was not detected, the alarm will not be initiated and so there is no further branching on that line in this example.

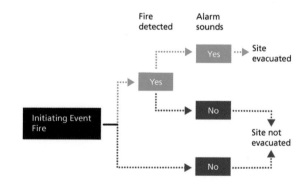

By using probability data, the event tree can be quantified.

ITEM	COMPONENT	FAILURE MODE	EFFECT	RPN	ACTION REQUIRED

FMEA table

What-if

In 'what-if' analysis of risk realisation, the assessor asks, "what if", and then digs deeper to look at the true potential of an incident. If we use a loss of containment of a flammable liquid as an example, the hazard is the flammable liquid, the potential event is the loss of containment (eg through gasket failure) and the resulting event could be identified as a spill. However, using hazard realisation, the assessor would look to identify the full potential of such an incident: the spillage could ignite, resulting in fire and/or explosion and damage/injury/fatality.

6. Concept of as low as is reasonably practicable (ALARP)

Unfortunately, it is impossible to reduce all risks to zero; the intention of the risk assessment and implementation of control measures/activities is to reduce the process risks to as low as reasonably practicable (ALARP). In practice, ALARP means that the risk has not just been reduced, but is now at the lowest level that can be achieved without incurring disproportionate costs. These costs can be not only financial, but also time, effort and inconvenience. When regulators make it a requirement to reduce risks to ALARP, they are setting a goal and leaving some flexibility in how to achieve it to the operator. With simpler processes, it is relatively easy to select risk controls, but with higher-hazard installations, information on what is considered ALARP will come from the use of the thorough risk assessment processes, best practice and guidance. This decision usually arises out of a cost-benefit analysis whereby the potential impact (the level of process safety risk) is weighed up against the cost of implementation, in order to determine the most appropriate course of action.

7. Hierarchy of risk controls

When deciding on risk controls, there is a hierarchy of options available that are placed in order of preference, with the most effective at the top and the least effective at the bottom. The NEBOSH syllabus for this course outlines the following:

- inherent safety;

- elimination (including minimised inventories);

- substitution;

- engineering controls (including segregation and spacing of process plant);

- administrative controls (procedural/behavioural).

We will now consider each of these in turn.

Inherent safety

The HSE commissioned an offshore safety report called Improving Inherent Safety[4], which described inherent safety as "a fundamental approach to hazard management which emphasised avoiding or eliminating the hazard at source rather than relying on add-on safety features or management systems and procedures to control them".

In the process industry, the need to have hazardous substances and workers in close proximity is often unavoidable, but the process can be made inherently safer by design, eg by segregating accommodation modules from production modules, or by locating office buildings away from production areas, rather than relying on active safety systems, such as fire deluge systems and evacuation procedures which, in the case of Piper Alpha, failed catastrophically.

Elimination and minimised inventories

It is sometimes possible to eliminate a hazardous process step or substance if the risk arising is considered too great. There are many examples, but an example in the process industry could be the purchase of a pre-mixed chemical rather than handling hazardous raw materials or subcontracting work to a competent contractor. It may also be possible to improve safety by reducing the quantity of hazardous materials stored on site through improved inventory management, eg rather than holding large tanks of solvent, an improved supply chain could guarantee delivery and maintain stock levels, although this would have to be balanced against, say, the risks from an increased number of offloading operations.

Risk management techniques used within the process industries

Substitution

Some chemicals can be substituted for a less hazardous alternative - rather than using a low flash point solvent, it may be possible to use a higher flash point material that poses less of a fire risk.

Engineering controls including segregation

Engineering controls include add-on solutions that improve the safety of the process. Suitable examples include the addition of ventilation and extraction systems to reduce the concentration of vapours in the atmosphere, enclosures to contain processes or segregated and protected control rooms to protect the operators. Hazardous processes can also be segregated from occupied areas, or storage vessels placed in separate locations to keep reactive chemicals apart. For example, at the Kennedy Space Centre in Florida, the storage vessel for the liquid oxygen is on the northwest corner of the launch pad, while the liquid hydrogen is stored on the northeast corner.

Administrative controls (procedural/ behavioural)

While administrative controls such as procedures, permit-to-work and training remain important, it is widely accepted that these are less effective than engineered controls, as they rely on the actions of individuals, ie human and organisation factors. Piper Alpha, while resulting from design and engineering flaws, had at the heart of the disaster, a failure in the procedural controls that were in place to manage maintenance and isolations. These activities are usually covered by a permit-to-work and this will be considered later in this element.

Finally, despite the best efforts of designers, engineers, permit co-ordinators and managers, sometimes people choose to break the rules or deviate from accepted practices. These behaviours can result in serious safety incidents and, therefore, effective training and supervision is essential to maintain a safe production unit. As we covered in Element 1, process safety leadership is essential to ensure that all workers are aware of their role and the required safety standards.

Allied Colloids, Bradford, fire and explosion incident.
©*Crown Copyright, Health and Safety Executive*

ELEMENT 1

ELEMENT 2

ELEMENT 3

ELEMENT 4

Asset management and maintenance strategies

1. Consideration of integrity standards

Whenever process equipment is designed or specified, it is essential that all of the intended activities are considered, eg not only must a pump be fit-for-purpose in that it supplies at the required pressure and flow rate, but it must also be suitable for the substance that it is transporting, be able to be cleaned, isolated (chemically, electrically and mechanically) for maintenance, safely removed and reinstated. When specifying equipment, consideration should be given to design standards, such as EN standards, or process safety standards, such as pipe pressure ratings or welding standards, eg Pressure Equipment (Safety) Regulations 2016, etc. This means that expert advice may be needed to ensure that the correct decisions are made at the design stage.

Wherever possible, inspection and visual maintenance should be possible without affecting the safe operation of the equipment, eg without removing covers and guards. Where isolations are required, these should be included at the design stage, eg by including lockable electrical isolators and inclusion of drain valves to allow 'double block and bleed' isolations.

> **KEY TERM**
>
> **Double block and bleed**
>
> The process of isolating a chemical or process line by closing and locking, or tagging two inline valves and opening a drain/vent line between them. This ensures that any leaks are to a safe location and not the open end of the line where work is carried out.

2. Consequences of failing to manage the integrity of assets

> **KEY TERMS**
>
> **Asset**
>
> An item of equipment, or an area of production plant.
>
> **Asset integrity**
>
> The ability of the equipment (asset) to operate as intended effectively and efficiently over its entire lifespan while ensuring the health and safety of those exposed to it, including the environment.

If assets are not maintained correctly, this can result in defects and failures that can have serious health and safety implications. For example:

- damaged, wearing or defective equipment can fail and cause leaks;

- equipment can fail, which can affect the performance of the process plant, eg failure of a hot oil system could cause the process to fail; loss of a cooling system could result in a runaway reaction;

- process plant will become ineffective and production will suffer;

- safety systems, such as fire suppression, may fail to operate correctly when required.

It is far more effective to maintain equipment on a preventive basis, rather than allowing it to become worn to the point of breakdown, and so an effective asset integrity management programme is essential for any plant.

Corroded and leaking pipework can lead to loss of containment.
©*Crown Copyright, Health and Safety Executive*

3. Selection of equipment for the operating environment

Some operating environments are such that use of the incorrect equipment can cause serious safety implications. For example, in a potentially flammable atmosphere where vapours or dusts can result in fire or explosion, the selection of the correct ATEX approved equipment is essential.

Asset management and maintenance strategies

KEY TERM

ATEX

'ATEX' is commonly used to refer to the two EU directives that control explosive atmospheres. It is from the French title of the 94/9/EC directive: Appareils destinés à être utilisés en ATmosphères EXplosibles, and ATEX-approved equipment that is suitable for use in an explosive atmosphere is given the following symbol:

In other circumstances, the atmosphere may damage the equipment. For example, equipment used outside should be correctly rated for water resistance, and in an atmosphere where there could be corrosive chemicals present, or even salty atmospheres, then any exposed metalwork could become corroded unless treated.

THOUGHT PROVOKER

Where on your site is there the potential for a flammable atmosphere? Are the areas clearly marked? Do you control the use of electrical equipment in that area to prevent ignition?

4. Asset integrity throughout the life cycle

The life-cycle phases of the asset integrity management system are defined as follows:

Phase 1 - Design

The objective is to design for safety and integrity throughout the life cycle of the process. This will require actions such as:

- safety studies;

- maintenance and inspection strategies;

- design, maintenance, inspection and operation philosophies;

- design review by verifier.

Phase 2 - Procurement, construction, installation and testing

The objective is to build in accordance with the design and with quality assurance to ensure that the build is completed correctly. Key actions include:

- developing purchasing and quality plans;

- obtaining inspection and test records;

- document completion and handover.

Phase 3 - Commissioning

The objectives include functional testing to demonstrate that the design standards were achieved and that the process performs as intended. Key actions include:

- commissioning and functional testing against design standards;

- sign-off of tests by commissioning engineers;

- verification by an external competent person;

- handover to operations.

Phase 4 - Operations

The objective here is to operate the plant within design intent. Key deliverables include:

- ongoing risk assessment;

- maintenance and inspection;

- monitoring of control measures;

- verification.

Phase 5 - Modifications

The objective is to ensure that modifications are carried out in a planned, properly-documented and risk-assessed manner, including identifying additional hazards and potential effects on operating and maintenance procedures, written schemes of examinations, as well as additional measures/actions are taken to ensure risks remain ALARP. Key deliverables here hinge on the use of an appropriate management of change process (covered elsewhere in this element).

Phase 6 - Decommissioning

This would entail the removal of the installation from operation. Key deliverables here would include:

- safety studies;

- development of decommissioning strategies;

- development of a decommissioning plan.

5. Plant maintenance documentation

Maintenance records will need to be retained carefully - some of these are required locally but some, for example the statutory records of pressure systems, legionella control, LEV testing and lifting equipment may be legally required. Records can be paper or electronic but must be traceable.

6. Risk-based maintenance and inspection strategy

There are three main types of maintenance and inspection strategies available:

- **Breakdown maintenance:**

  this is highly reactive and relies on the operator repairing or replacing plant and equipment that has failed while in use. It is not preventive in that, the only indication the operator has that there is a problem, is the failure of the equipment;

- **Condition monitoring:**

  in this maintenance strategy, the operator looks at indicators that could demonstrate that the equipment is not, or will not be, working as intended - this picks up symptoms of the deterioration before the equipment actually fails. For example, motors can be monitored for noise levels to determine if the bearings are worn, thermography (thermal imaging cameras) can be used to detect hot spots on equipment, which can indicate areas that may be overheating;

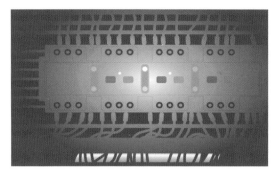

Thermal imaging used to identify hot spots on equipment.

- **Planned preventive maintenance:**

  this is a truly proactive maintenance system whereby inspections and checks are carried out before failures occur, to minimise the risk of plant impact. A true planned preventive maintenance system includes periodic inspection, planned maintenance activities, non-destructive testing and actions to correct any deficiencies that are identified.

ACTIVITY

Identify five planned preventive maintenance activities that could be carried out on a site.

Risk-based calibration of instrumentation

Instrument calibration is an essential activity in the process industries and there are many good reasons to calibrate instrumentation, but the consequences of neglecting to maintain calibration can cause:

- failure to meet the quality system;

- safety risks for employees and customers;

- poor product quality and loss of reputation;

- failure to comply with legislation, causing the loss of the licence to operate;

- unexpected downtime;

- economic losses.

The accuracy of measurement of instruments drifts over time and usually it is very difficult to eliminate this drift. Modern instruments typically drift less than older models but environmental conditions, extreme temperatures, changing seasons and humidity can cause stress on the instruments and those that are used more often or in critical processes tend to wear out more quickly.

Asset management and maintenance strategies

Instrumentation Technician calibrating digital flow meter.

Other instrumentation is used to ensure workers can enter confined spaces and work in safety (oxygen and gas detectors) whilst voltage detectors ensure electricians can work confidently on equipment that has been isolated and locked off.

Temporary pressure gauges ensure the integrity of pressure vessels and pipelines during shut-down maintenance, pneumatic and hydrostatic testing.

Risk-based thinking is nowadays applied to the calibration of instrumentation, essentially calculating the legal, human and financial cost to the company if the calibration programme fails.

The most common procedure is for users to check instruments periodically to see if they have drifted and make adjustments as necessary, but if operators don't have a policy in place to ensure instrumentation is routinely calibrated, and the instrument drifts, it is not able to perform the measurement with assured accuracy.

Calibration of instrumentation is of paramount importance because instrumentation is responsible for ensuring the plant operates within its safe operating envelope, monitoring aspects such as process flow, temperature, pressure and pH Levels. Maintenance procedures must be established to ensure instrumentation sensors and transmitters are calibrated, with an appropriate audit trail.

As an example, hydrocarbon leak detectors (usually gas detectors) have to be maintained and calibrated to ensure that any threat to the safety of the process and/or workers is detected in good time and either neutralised or mitigated.

Process plants must also constantly monitor their emissions to meet environmental compliance obligations. Emissions monitoring and measuring equipment has to be shown to be accurate to prove that set targets are being met, and the only way to show this is through regular calibration. Failure to meet these obligations may cause damage to the environment and bring prosecutions and/or fines and, in a worst-case scenario, the plant may be shut down or lose their licence to operate.

Role, purpose and features of a permit-to-work system

1. Purpose and effective use

KEY TERMS

Permit-to-work system

A formal, documented procedure that forms part of a safe system of work. It is commonly used for high-risk work and it documents measures to reduce risks, such as isolations. It is used to ensure that the correct precautions are in place and that all those who need to know about the work are informed.

A permit-to-work is used commonly for high-risk activities, such as:

- hot work;

- work on complex plant that requires isolation (chemical, electrical, mechanical or gas);

- confined space entry;

- work on high-voltage electrical systems;

- excavations near buried services.

The permit is only part of the safe system of work and is used in combination with method statements and task analysis or risk assessments. The permit issuer requires a detailed knowledge of the plant where the work is to be carried out, and the workers use the method statements and task analysis to communicate the hazards and controls needed to the issuer.

2. Key features of permit-to-work

The permit-to-work contains the following key features:

- scope of work - this specifies what work is to be carried out, the location and the equipment to be worked on;

- duration of the work - this includes the date and time that the permit is valid to and from;

- identification of hazards - the known hazards identified through the risk assessment and from site knowledge are detailed; Any specific risk assessments can be referenced;

- isolations - any isolations needed (such as electrical, mechanical or chemical lines) are detailed and the location of the isolation recorded; This should follow a formal lock out, tag out (LOTO) process that physically prevents the re-energisation of the system; Any additional controls, such as PPE, are also detailed;

- links to other permits - if there are other permits related to the activities, these are also referenced here; For example, there may be a confined space permit for parts of the activities;

- emergency controls - any additional emergency controls are detailed;

- specific controls - any additional controls, such as gas testing requirements and PPE needed, are recorded here;

- permit acceptance and cancellation - in this section, the permit is handed from issuer to worker before the job commences; Both parties sign to confirm their understanding of the contents and their agreement that they will work to the permit conditions; On completion of the work, the permit is handed back and cancelled; The sections are as follows:

  - issue - the permit is signed by the issuer to confirm that the isolations are in place and that the responsibility for the area is being handed to the accepter;

  - receipt - the permit is signed by the person(s) doing the work to confirm that they understand and abide by the conditions;

  - clearance/return to service - the permit is signed by the worker to state that the work is complete and the area can be returned to service, or that work is not yet complete and needs to be continued. This hands the area back to the operator;

  - cancellation - the operator signs to confirm that they are in agreement that the plant can be returned to service and that the isolations are removed.

Sometimes, permits are issued in triplicate, with one copy displayed at the job site, one copy given to the worker and the final master copy remaining in the permit office. It is essential that the person issuing the permit has good knowledge of the area and also does not issue another permit-to-work in the area that could clash. It should also be remembered that a permit is just a document - if it is not issued correctly and treated with the respect needed, then it will offer no protection from harm.

Role, purpose and features of a permit-to-work system

3. Interfaces with adjacent plant

It is essential that the permit issuer considers the potential impact of the works on adjacent plant or equipment, or the possibility that other plant could affect the safe operation of the permit. Equally, if the installation has duty and stand-by plant, then controls must be in place to ensure that these are not worked on simultaneously. This is often achieved by ensuring all permits are issued from a central issuing authority or location, and displayed clearly so that any clashes can be identified - at a simple level, it would be dangerous to issue a permit to carry out hot work in the vicinity of work to remove and replace equipment containing flammable materials.

4. Interfaces with contractors

The permit-to-work process is intended to protect contractors and workers alike - both should be issued with permits where appropriate, although contractors may also be required to take additional measures, eg attend contractor inductions or prove competency. Permits should always be issued by the organisation and never by the contractors themselves.

> **THOUGHT PROVOKER**
>
> Is there a permit-to-work in use at your workplace? Have a look at it and see how each of the sections we have discussed are included in the permit.

5. Types of permit

There are several different types of permit-to-work that may be in use.

Isolation permit/general permit-to-work

This contains the details of general work activities such as those requiring lock out and isolation of electrical, mechanical or chemical services. It is often known simply as a 'permit-to-work' and may form the basis on which others are written.

Hot work permit

These are issued when the work could generate a spark or hot surface, and there is, therefore, a risk of ignition. The specific controls may include clearing the area of combustibles, fire-watching, control of flammable vapours and use of screens and fire blankets.

Cold work

Some work can generate a risk of ignition without being classically considered 'hot work'; for want of a better term, this is known as 'cold work'. For example, drilling, cutting metal, use of metal equipment, eg Hickson & Welch incident, etc can generate sparks and small localised heat sources, but would not fall under the definition of hot work as there is no flame or glowing surface.

Electrical

Work on high voltage (HV) electrical systems is usually controlled by a special permit-to-work, as this can only be issued by authorised persons who are suitably qualified. Those accepting HV permits must also be competent, and controls may include specific complex disconnection, isolation and lock off requirements.

Confined space

Work in confined spaces is usually carried out under permit, with additional requirements detailed, which will include the methods used to assure a respirable atmosphere, any gas monitoring requirements, emergency and rescue procedures, etc.

Benefits and limitations of electronic and paper-based systems

The HSE document HSG250 - *Guidance on permit-to-work systems - "A guide for the petroleum, chemical and allied industries"*, gives good guidance on this subject and states that *"Permits can be produced electronically and a number of companies are using this type of system. There may be advantages in reducing the amount of paperwork associated with the permit process. However, before introducing electronic permit system operators must be sure that a suitable system (eg password-protected electronic signatures) is in place to:*

* *prevent unauthorised issue or acceptance;*

* *permits cannot be issued remotely without a site visit;*

* *systems are in place to prevent permits already issued from being altered without the alterations being communicated to all concerned;*

* *the facility exists for paper permits to be produced for display at the job site;*

- *training is provided to ensure that operators assess the specific job and do not rely on 'cutting and pasting' existing sections from other permits;*

- *suitable back-up systems are available in the event of a software failure or power outage."*

Whatever media are employed at a particular site or installation, paper-based or electronic, it is essential that the particular use and types of permit are clear to everyone involved or affected by potentially hazardous work.

6. Typical circumstances when a permit is not required

If the activities are not on live process plant, do not require isolation or disconnection, and do not fall under the other permit activity definitions (ie not hot work or confined space) then this will not usually be carried out under permit-to-work. Instead, another safe system of work will be used. Examples include activities involving routine production and first-line maintenance carried out by operations personnel, such as topping up oil, water or tuning controllers.

Normally, the activities of inspectors, surveyors, engineers and visitors will also not require a permit-to-work, provided their presence in the operational area is approved in advance and their activity does not interfere with plant or equipment and they are not carrying potential ignition sources.

Work carried out in designated maintenance (for example, workshops) and construction areas generally do not require a permit to work.

Electrical technicians review a work permit issued to them on an oil and gas platform.

Safe shift handover

A shift handover is the term used to describe the transfer of information between a shift who are leaving work and the incoming new shift. The Piper Alpha disaster in 1988 was caused, in a large part, by the failure to hand information over from one shift to another. In an HSE publication, it was said that "There was a breakdown in communications and the permit-to-work system at shift changeover and safety procedures were not practised sufficiently". This all too tragically illustrated the importance of ensuring that safety critical information is reliably passed from one shift to another. There are many types of safety critical information that need to be passed from one shift to another - issues from the previous shift, safety incidents, and ongoing works with any permits that are open and being worked on. It is, therefore, essential that shift handover is given an appropriate level of significance.

1. Two-way and joint responsibility

We have seen that shift handovers are safety critical communications, and they are the joint responsibility of both the outgoing and incoming shift leaders. Both must contribute to the discussions and be receptive to, and understand, the information shared.

2. Competence

Those carrying out shift handovers must have the right level of technical knowledge and expertise, but also be able to communicate effectively. This may mean that communications training is needed to improve the skillset of the workers.

3. Shift handover requirements

Shift handover should be:

- considered a high priority: it may be necessary, for instance, to bring the incoming shift in a bit earlier to ensure that there is time for the discussions;

- carried out face-to-face between those involved: this is usually between the shift leaders;

- carried out using accurate written and verbal communication: the handovers are usually supported by documentation to record the discussions (eg handover log);

- based on analysis of the information needs of the incoming staff: there are some activities that would be essential to communicate to the incoming teams, eg if the sprinkler system was not working or if critical spares were due to site;

- given as much time as necessary to allow for questioning, explanation and clarification.

Shift handovers are particularly important:

- during plant maintenance, which is carried across two shifts;

- when shifts or team members have been absent for a long period;

- when safety critical systems are not operational or have been over-ridden, eg when sprinkler systems are isolated for maintenance.

4. Typical information shared at shift handover

As we have seen earlier, it is essential that shift handover is given an appropriate level of significance. In some instances, there may be a need to physically demonstrate the status of the plant or process to the incoming shift to ensure that there is a clear understanding of any issues or limitations arising from ongoing works, for example.

Typical examples of information shared during shift handover

The main issues communicated at shift handover include:

- operational status of the plant;

- any emergency situations or incidents that have occurred;

- any safety issues, particularly safety systems that are not operating/are isolated;

- details of maintenance activities, especially any ongoing works that will continue into the next shift;

- maintenance activities planned for the incoming shift;

- permit-to-work details, especially those still open;

- operational issues for the incoming shift (eg production plans);

- planned receipt of hazardous material deliveries for the incoming shift;

- any drills or exercises planned;

- physical demonstration of plant state.

Contractor management

1. The scale of contractor use within the process industries

A 'contractor' is an individual or organisation that is paid to provide a service to a client without them being directly employed. The scale of contractor use within the process industries is significant, with many organisations using contractors to deliver the following types of service:

- provision of additional manpower and labour, eg during high production or busy maintenance periods;

- provision of specialist skills, eg during construction and shut-down activities. This could include contracted designers through to provision of welders, electricians and pipe fitters to install the plant and equipment. Diving services, transfer vessels and catering companies can also often be found as contractors to a larger organisation.

ACTIVITY

Identify different types of contractor/contract organisation who could be on site.

---

2. Contractor selection

It is important to carefully select contractors and appoint on the basis of their competence rather than for convenience. Clients can be held liable for the actions of contractors if they do not take enough care in properly selecting them. Contractors need to be capable of delivering the works safely and should have adequate experience of the process industry to ensure that they understand the potential impact of their work on the site and, in particular, any operational plant or processes.

Contractor selection

The following criteria can be used to assess the suitability of a contractor:

- experience in the type of work required, and experience of working within the process industry (as the hazards of the process industry may be substantially different from construction sites, for instance);

- trained and experienced in specific safety requirements of the environment, eg offshore requirements may include specific offshore survival training, etc;

- suitability of the organisation's health and safety policy;

- suitability and quality of their risk assessments; examples could be requested for assessment purposes;

- suitability and level of detail provided in method statements;

- accident history and statistics, including first-aid and near-miss reporting;

- enforcement history and prosecutions;

- details of how health and safety performance is monitored on site, including site inspections;

- qualifications of workers throughout the organisation, including competency or site cards for workers and the health and safety qualifications of managers and health and safety advisers;

- membership of a professional body or trade association;

- procedures for the selection and management of subcontractors;

- details and levels of insurance cover;

- arrangements for liaison with clients;

- references from previous clients.

3. Periodic review of contractor safety performance

It is important to maintain a close working relationship with contractors, and to be comfortable and satisfied with their safety performance. This will require regular reviews of the activities of contractors, which may include:

- carrying out site inspections to check compliance with the method statements and risk assessments;

- carrying out safety tours to monitor general standards, including housekeeping;

- attending regular meetings with contractors to discuss any issues and review accident data.

Contractor management

4. Contractor induction and obligations to provide information on site risks

While the information relating to site hazards may have been provided initially at the tender stage, it is essential that all of the relevant information is communicated to the individual workers. This is usually carried out by the use of a site induction. The site induction is a training and awareness session provided for all contractors working on a site, and includes information such as:

- sign in/out procedures;

- emergency procedures (fire, first aid, gas release, etc);

- site rules, such as transport safety, smoking, work at height rules, etc;

- specific site hazards, eg flammable atmospheres, chemicals, asbestos;

- PPE requirements;

- permit-to-work requirements;

- accident reporting procedures;

- near-miss and hazard reporting, etc.

The client is best placed to advise the contractors on the potentially unique hazards and risks posed due to work on the site. This information should be provided at the tender stage to ensure all parties are aware of the hazards of the site and any implications that this may have on the work. For example, if work were to be carried out on a vessel that had previously been in service, then the client would need to provide details of not only the working environment (eg is there a flammable atmosphere, is the work at height, etc) but also details of the previous use of the vessel, together with any information on the past contents (eg safety data sheets). Other hazards may include the presence of asbestos, overhead or underground services, etc.

A supervisor discusses a work task with a contractor.
©*Crown Copyright, Health and Safety Executive*

5. Contractor ownership and site supervision/representation

When contractors are used on site, they can be affected by the activities carried out by the site workers. As a result, they should be included in process risk assessments and safe systems of work. There should be clearly identified persons responsible in place, for the approval and day-to-day management of the contractors for the client, to ensure that they are well managed and supported. Each contractor should know who their client contact is, as they will be the person responsible for answering any questions relating to the job.

6. Auditing contractor performance

Contractors in any workplace need to be assessed to ensure that they are capable of carrying out the work, and monitored to ensure that they are working to the agreed health and safety standards. This is even more important in the process industry, as the risks are so much greater if the control is not correct.

The initial assessment should be carried out based on the method statements provided. Checks could include reviewing to ensure that the standards meet legal requirements, and also follow accepted guidance, such as that published by the HSE.

During the work, the contractors' working practices should be monitored to ensure that they adhere to the conditions of the method statements. This includes the monitoring of the standards that were described at the tender stage to ensure that the promised actions are being adhered to in practice at the job site. While the decision to deviate from the agreed procedures could be seen to be the responsibility of the contractor, this could result in endangering workers from the contract company and the client, and so the maintenance of appropriate standards remains a joint responsibility.

After the work has been completed, the client and contractor should meet in order to review the standard of work and also the manner in which the work was carried out, including the accident history and other contractor performance measures.

7. Contractor handover to client

Finally, once the work is completed, any plant, buildings or equipment installed will need to be handed over to the client. Where there has been an installation, the level of information required to be handed over on completion may be dictated by legislation; however, information that may be needed could include:

- operation and maintenance manuals;
- pipework and instrumentation diagrams;
- updated layout plans, including location of services;
- design specifications;
- as-built drawings.

Contractors may also need to hand back any plant and equipment after work, through the cancellation of any permits-to-work that were opened for the job.

Housing/siting of contractors

A defining aspect of the explosion and fire at the BP Texas City refinery in 2005 is that, although tragically, 15 contract employees working in or near the trailers sited between the ISOM and the NDU unit were killed, a total of 180 workers at the refinery were also injured, 66 seriously enough that they had days away from work. Of the seriously injured, only 14 were BP employees. The rest were contractor employees from 13 different firms. Of the 114 workers given first aid, 35 were BP employees; 79 were contract employees from 14 different contracting firms. It was also established that none of the contract workers in the area surrounding the ISOM were essential to the start-up of the unit (Baker Panel Report).

What was demonstrated in the Texas City incident is that 'temporary' accommodation, such as trailers and huts for contractors, become permanent and do not feature in the management of change process or any form of Process Hazard Analysis of the overall site during major works.

To address the potential safety and health hazards of new buildings introduced, such as temporary mobile office trailers used in unit turnarounds, process operators should evaluate all newly sited structures under its management of change procedure and they should also be included in the overall Process Hazard Analysis (PHA).

Temporary accommodation for workers (either permanent employees or contractors) should be based on exclusion zones for areas where explosions are possible and all occupied trailers should be located outside of vulnerable areas, even if this means moving them beyond the boundary of the facility.

It might be noted that a large number of Texas City workers were relocated to a permanent building away from the refinery after the incident.

Each contractor present on site should be aware of who their client contact is.
©Crown Copyright, Health and Safety Executive

Practice questions and references

References

1. HSG254 Developing process safety indicators: A step-by-step guide for chemical and major hazard industries, HSE, 2006

2. INDG163 Risk Assessment - a brief guide to controlling risks in the workplace, HSE, 2014

3. HSE Information Sheet: Guidance on Risk Assessment for Offshore Installations - Offshore Information Sheet No. 3/2006

4. Improving inherent safety, prepared by AEA Technology and Loughborough Consultants for the HSE, 1996

Practice questions

Q1. Process organisations have in place a wide range of mitigation measures designed to reduce the consequences of a major incident. Which risk management technique is especially suited to assess the effectiveness of these mitigation measures?

A   Failure Mode Effects Analysis (FMEA).

B   Event tree analysis (ETA).

C   Risk assessment (RA).

D   Hazard Identification (HAZID).

Q2. Which of the following is an example of planned preventive maintenance?

A   Daily visual inspections of process plant.

B   Greasing of pump bearings.

C   Regular sampling of product.

D   Testing of stack emissions.

Q3. Quantitative risk assessment differs from qualitative risk assessment because it is more:

A   adaptive.

B   objective.

C   subjective.

D   detective.

Q4. A preferred method of conducting a shift handover is:

A   face to face using verbal and written communication.

B   by telephone using verbal communication.

C   via a log book using written communication.

D   by radio using verbal communication.

Q5. Which of the following is the most important consideration when selecting contractors?

A Proving that they have no previous or pending enforcement actions.

B Providing method statements, risk assessments and safety policies.

C Evidence of previous safe working and understanding their impact on others.

D Membership of a professional body and adequate insurance cover for the work.

Q6. Two separate work permits had been issued for the maintenance work on a pump. One was for repair of the pump and one was for removal and servicing of the pressure relief valve on the discharge side of the pump. The pump repair had been completed but the servicing of the pressure relief valve had not been completed by the end of the shift. In place of the pressure relief valve a 'blank' had been loosely installed. During shift handover, the maintenance work and return to service of the pump was discussed, but no mention was made of the servicing work being carried out on its pressure relief valve. The pump was then started, allowing flammable liquids to leak from the 'blank'. This vapour cloud ignited, causing a fire.

Which of the following actions during shift handover would have been most effective in preventing this accident?

A Verbal communication in a quiet place between incoming and outgoing workers.

B Confirmation of permits signed off as completed.

C Discussion of the recorded process checks undertaken by the outgoing workers.

D A physical demonstration of the plant state between incoming and outgoing workers.

Process safety hazard control

Tank farm and supporting infrastructure.

This element focuses on the purpose and requirements of operating procedures and explores the hazards and risks associated with different components of the process industries.

Learning outcomes

On completion of this element, you should be able to:

3.1 Explain the purpose and requirements of standard operating procedures.

3.2 Outline the controls that should be adopted to control the safe start-up and shut-down of process plant.

3.3 Outline the necessity for performance standards for safety critical systems and equipment and the concept of 'FARSI'.

3.4 Outline the hazards and controls associated with the use of steam and water within the process industries.

3.5 Outline the hazards and controls associated with electricity/static electricity within the process industries.

3.6 Outline the physical forms of dangerous substances and how these can determine process risk.

3.7 Outline the hazards presented by chemical reactions and the protective measures used to mitigate the consequences of a thermal runaway reaction.

3.8 Outline the hazards and controls available for the bulk storage of dangerous substances.

Operating procedures

1. What is a safe operating envelope?

When designing any process plant, particularly where the process, the materials being used, the product being produced and the reactions taking place are hazardous, the design needs to be such as to prevent the hazards being out of control.

To do this, the designer aims to ensure that the process itself is controlled within certain limits, to prevent a hazardous situation developing. The expression safe operating envelope refers to the limits of the operating conditions under which the process can take place safely. Typically, process limits are established by setting upper and lower levels for a range of parameters. Providing the process reaction takes place within these limits, it will operate safely, all else being equal. The common process parameters are temperature, pressure and volume but, depending on the process, may also include properties such as pH, conductivity, level, flow (rates) composition, mixing (agitation), etc

A storage tank, for example, will be designed and built to withstand the pressure exerted by the contents, and also when empty (should a vacuum occur). So, as long as the filling/emptying of the tank ensures that the maximum and minimum internal pressures are not breached, the tank will remain intact and there will be no escape of hazardous material. The operating limits that define the safe operating envelope may be taken from manufacturers' specifications, operating experience and theoretical calculations. So, the safe operating envelope is a short way of referring to the design parameters that define the safe operation of the process; operating outside this safe operating envelope implies that a dangerous state may be produced that could have disastrous consequences. Wherever possible, the safe operating envelope should have as wide margins as possible to allow for the inevitable fluctuation that occurs in normal operation processing. For example, if the safe operating pressure is defined in terms of an upper and lower limit that are close together, then there is very little scope for inherent variation and the safe operating envelope will be more critical as it will be generally harder to maintain the pressure within the safe operating limits. If the pressure difference between the lower and upper limit is reasonably large, then the safe operating envelope is consequently more robust as it allows for a wider fluctuation.

Understanding the safe operating envelope has implications for the required monitoring of the process elements, and for the application of emergency responses. When the envelope is breached or likely to be breached, eg the fitting of pressure relief valves (see explosion protection systems in element 4.2). It also describes for the operator the process criteria within which to contain the reactions being undertaken.

The terms pressure relief valve (PRV) and pressure safety valve (PSV) are often used interchangeably to describe a valve that is located on a vessel under pressure (and, in some cases, a vessel that could become pressurised). The term PRV, according to some authorities, should be used to describe a relief device on a liquid filled vessel that opens gradually in proportion to any increase in pressure over the pre-set pressure (below the designed maximum operating pressure of the vessel). The increased pressure may be the result of a variation in normal operations or a safety event, such as exposure of the vessel to fire. Whereas, PSV describes a relief valve device fitted to a vessel containing a compressible fluid or gas, which opens fully and suddenly when the set pressure of the valve is reached. Whichever expression is used, the purpose of such valves is to relieve excess pressure that otherwise might expose the vessel to rupture, taking it outside the safe operating envelope. Once the pressure in the vessel is stabilised to a safe operating pressure, the valve closes. The discharge from the PRV/PSV will be released either into the environment or into a holding or pipeline, depending on the circumstances and the contents of the vessel.

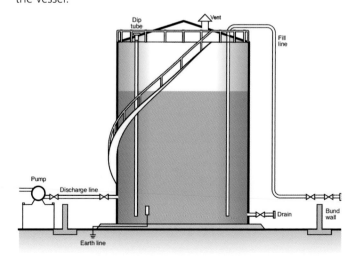

Source: HSE176 - Storage of flammable liquids in tanks, 2015

2. Operating procedures: purpose, types, and who should be involved

Purpose of operating procedures

The purpose of a process standard operating procedure (SOP) is to cover three main areas:

1. Safety considerations associated with the process. This is to inform the operator of the safety hazards associated with all of the materials used in the process. The operator needs to be thoroughly familiar with the potential safety and environmental hazards associated with plant operation, and understand the process flowsheet and how the plant is designed and operates. This will include process interlocks and when they might be activated, location of pressure relief valves, rupture disks, gauges, etc and where discharges go to when releases occur.

2. The description of the control system. How the safety instrumentation system (SIS) and the proportional-integral-derivative (PID) controllers operate, and if and when manual operation may be required or set points adjusted.

3. A description of standard operating conditions and the options available to operators to optimally adjust the process when there is an excursion from the standard conditions. This is essential to avoid radical shut-downs or overruns and uneconomic operation, while at the same time working within the safety envelope.

KEY TERMS

Safety instrumentation system (SIS)

The system for connections and equipment that operates automatically the process controls, such as valves and maintains the process in the operational envelope.

Proportional-integral-derivative (PID)

The three separate elements - proportional-integral-derivative - which comprise the control loop that regulates the process variables, eg pressure. This avoids the need to have manually operated process control.

In essence, a standard operating procedure (SOP) is a documented step-by-step explanation/instruction on how to conduct specific parts of the operating process. It sets out the way a certain task or activity is done so that mistakes (either in action or timing, and sometimes both) which might lead to a situation where the safe operating envelope could be breached are avoided. For example, the addition of a chemical feedstock into a process line may involve a complex understanding of which lines to open, which valves to close and the volume and flow rate of the feed into a reaction vessel. If the wrong action is carried out, the consequences could be disastrous, or they may simply lead to a rejection of below-standard product. As far as process safety goes, the SOP will focus on the reaction status (the chemical reaction), results of the Process Hazard Analysis (PHA) and expert knowledge of the dangers that may ensue if an operational procedure is carried out incorrectly. The overall purpose of the SOP is to identify and maintain the operating parameters (measures) such as pressure limits, temperature ranges, flow rates, etc, at the required 'safe' levels. Creating a standard operating procedure is a way to remove variation in work performance caused by people who may complete the same work tasks in different ways.

The SOP may also include, where relevant, occupational safety issues, such as manual handling, worker exposure to chemicals, use of PPE, etc In addition to this, the SOP provides a template for the training required to ensure that the operator is both familiar with the range of SOPs and competent to successfully apply particular SOPs.

SOPs provide a means of communicating the expected operational procedures to all stakeholders. They also provide a means of capturing specific plant, equipment and operational detail that maintains knowledge of various process elements. This prevents the reliance on individual memory, particularly useful when the operators change or leave the plant.

Types of operating procedures

Typical SOPs will cover such matters as:

- start-up/shut-down of a process, or part of a process;

- plant and equipment maintenance (including changes and modifications to plant or equipment);

- responding to alarms tripping;

- filling, emptying and charging of vessels, pipelines and reactors;

Operating procedures

- responding to unplanned deviations and 'abnormal operations' that can arise because of: fluctuations in feedstock, the control system, general wear and tear before maintenance can be carried out, failure of instrumentation, failure of a control valve, or failure of a pump; for instance:

  - Trialling of variations in operations.
  - Responding to emergencies.
  - Management Of Change (MOC).

These procedures are generally prescriptive and mandatory, requiring a full or partial safety review if they are to be altered or varied.

In addition to procedures for maintaining the process safety envelope, there will also be procedures for handling 'software', such as providing guidance on how to carry out a safety review, delivery of training and maintenance of competence.

Who is involved in developing the procedures?

Traditionally, many safety incursions in process operations have been blamed on failings by operators, very often because the SOP has not been followed, is not accurate or does not exist. To overcome such problems, current high reliability organisation (HRO) theory and practice points to the involvement of experts in the design and writing of the SOPs. The experts include those actually doing the work, so in reality the initial writing and development of any SOP requires input from the designer/engineer and also the operator(s); in other words, the stakeholders involved with that part of the process to which the procedure relates. This latter is to ensure that the procedure actually matches what is done. During plant operations, procedures often come about as a result of operators finding alternative ways to achieve a task goal or having to deviate from the expected action because of design, architectural or environmental conditions. These procedures are rarely documented and, as a result, there may be serious safety consequences as the self-devised procedure does not take into account known risks or aberrant chemical reactions. Involving operators in the writing of procedures has been shown to be a positive action because people who participate in their formulation are much more likely to both accept and follow the procedure.

They have a sense of ownership in the process, are positive and generate ideas, which assist in ensuring the procedure will work in practice. When devising SOPs, the HSE states, "There should be no easier, more dangerous alternatives than following the procedure[1]". This implies a need to ensure human-factor aspects are covered when writing and training in the procedure. So, as part of a team approach to devising an SOP, a human factors (HF) expert might need to be consulted.

The development of SOP's should involve those actually undertaking the task.
©Crown Copyright, Health and Safety Executive

3. What should be included within operating procedures?

The procedure should cover such matters as:

- the purpose of the operation;

- the plant/equipment and materials being used;

- who does what, where, how and why;

- a description of the hazards and risks that the procedure is designed to deal with and that will arise if it is not followed. The hazards will include the chemicals and materials involved (liquids, solids (eg dusts), gases, fumes) and the parameters essential to safe operation, such as temperature, pressure flow rate, volumes, composition, etc.

It is important that operators are fully aware of both the hazards involved in the procedure, and the consequences if it is not followed. The procedure should also highlight the physical and engineering controls required, and the order in which they should be engaged, eg earthing of a receiving vessel where there is the possibility of static causing an explosion or fire when the vessel is being manually charged with feedstock:

- how to actually do the required task or activity, including the use of illustrations (pictures, photos, drawings), flowcharts and checklists;

- the authorisation of workers to carry out the procedure. This is usually achieved by training operators and ensuring supervision, when necessary, so that competence in the procedure is developed and maintained. Any requirement to wear appropriate PPE;

- availability and accessibility of spare parts, when appropriate, together with the necessary standard.

4. Requirement for procedures to be clearly understood

It is essential that every procedure can be understood and followed by the operator. In order to ensure this, it may be necessary to draft the procedure, trial it and then revise it until the procedure is both clear and easily followed. Any ambiguity or opportunity for incorrect actions to be taken when following the procedure will present a risk, both to the operator and to the process. One of the advantages of including operators in the drafting is that the likelihood for errors occurring will be reduced. However, it is also important that someone who is not familiar with the procedure demonstrates that it can actually be followed. Another important feature is to ensure the 'what' and 'how' of the SOP is supported by the 'why'. If management simply imposes the procedure, it is unlikely to be followed with the degree of rigour required. When operators are involved with the design of the procedure, they gain ownership of it and so are more likely to implement it as drafted. This is because they better understand why the steps have been arranged in the way they have, based on a full analysis of the hazards and risks and the possible variables that might otherwise occur.

EXAMPLE

When procedures are not fully understood, disasters can happen. Have a look at the following for examples of this, including the West Fertiliser Company incident in Texas:

www.csb.gov/videos

5. Ensuring operating procedures remain current and accurate

For a variety of reasons, procedures may become outdated or applied with a degree of laxity. One cause is human frailty, often summed up in the expression "familiarity breeds contempt". If the operator finds that missing a step or not applying part of the SOP is easier or quicker and there is no adverse consequence, then over time the SOP becomes 'revised'. This revised SOP is, of course, at variance with the intended SOP that was designed to keep both the process and the individual operator safe, for good reasons. This drift away from the designed SOP then becomes the common practice, but because it is not now based on an appropriate risk assessment, there is a grave likelihood that at some point the deviation from the expected SOP will have dangerous consequences.

Another reason for deviation will be gradual changes in plant and materials, eg a change in feedstock that has not triggered a management of change assessment (and hence a revision in the SOP) but has caused the operator to modify the way things are done, perhaps by reformulation of pellets to feed manually into a batch process that would make it easier for the operator to overfill the delivery bin.

To avoid these and other deviations, it is essential to ensure the SOP achieves its purpose of keeping the process and the operator safe. This involves reporting all deviations from the SOP for whatever reason, carrying out programmed reviews of the procedure and oversight of actual practice. Likewise, careful checking and monitoring of the SIS (linked to risk-based inspection) is an important adjunct to ensure that the process is operating as intended.

Operating procedures

Reporting and subsequent analysis of deviations from the expected process parameters, either as a result of direct observation or as a retrospective analysis (eg quality of end product) is essential to establish if the SOPs are, in fact, working, or if the variations being experienced are indicative of a potential loss of the safety envelope. Variations can be detected by:

- assessment of defect complaints;

- product out of specification;

- reports on deviations in the process;

- variations in yield, (both continuous and batch records);

- feedstock raw material records (usually by lab analysis);

- adverse event reports.

Verification can also be achieved by reviewing MOC reports, inspection records and reports, and frequency of maintenance on safety-critical plant and equipment.

The analysis of such variations and adverse events (or even good events that are not expected) should be both methodical and systematic and involve a team approach to lessen the chance for 'group think' to influence decisions on whether the SOPs involved are both accurate and relevant.

6. Limitations of procedures and consequences of deviating from them

There are several reasons why there may be limitation to the use of an SOP. From the drafting stage: while it is known that stakeholder involvement both improves the quality of the SOP and increases the likelihood that it will be adhered to, it is almost certain that not every relevant member of site workers will be able to participate in the drafting. The total involvement of relevant people in the SOP formulation and implementation is thus not practical and hence there is a limitation of the effectiveness of individual performance.

Again, for a variety of reasons, an SOP may be subject to local change or misuse: the development of an SOP for every operation results in a large number of documents (even if they are flowcharts) that operators will need to be familiar with and, depending on their competence, they may find too difficult to recall or select the appropriate SOP.

This then requires a focus on training and review for which there may be no time, given the constraints of process and product delivery. Factors that may affect the ability for operators to correctly apply the SOP include:

- time pressure;

- workload;

- staffing levels;

- training;

- supervision.

More importantly, the SOP approach assumes that humans are infallible when, in reality, human fallibility may mean that, in certain situations and at certain times, it is possible that the operator will deviate from the SOP.

Technical issues are also liable to limit the effectiveness of an SOP: it is impossible to identify all eventualities and the unexpected failure of plant or equipment may not be addressed in the SOPs in the circumstances in which the failure occurs.

The consequences of not correctly applying an SOP can vary from no significant outcome to major disaster. The 'no significant outcome' is often dangerous as it allows operatives to assume that because nothing adverse has happened on one or two occasions, the deviation from the SOP is unimportant. This allows for 'drift' to occur and, when repeated over time, can lead to a situation where a serious event occurs that takes the process outside the safe operating envelope.

The more obvious situation is, of course, when a failure to follow an SOP places the operator in danger or causes major consequences for both plant and workers, eg fire or explosion resulting from premature opening of a vessel containing pyrophoric iron sulphide.

Grosvenor Chemicals, Huddersfield, incident.
©*Crown Copyright, Health and Safety Executive*

Safe start-up and shut-down

Importance of responding to alarms

Serious industrial accidents can and do occur, and the near-meltdown of the nuclear reactor at Three Mile Island on March 28, 1979, is a case in point.

The incident was closely related to the poor design of the operator interface where a saturation of alarms confused operators for two and a half hours before they were able to understand the problem.

The control panel was huge, with hundreds of alarms, and some key indicators were placed in locations where the operators could not see them.

During the first few minutes of the accident, more than 100 alarms went off, and there was no system for suppressing the unimportant signals so that operators could concentrate on the significant alarms.

An alarm is an announcement to the operator to tell them a process variable (or measurement) has passed a defined limit and is approaching an undesirable or unsafe value. The announcement can include audible sounds, visual indications such as flashing lights, text or colour changes and other graphic or pictorial changes and messages. These indications announce that a problem requires the operators' action.

These alarms are an integral part of the process control system and the operator can either silence or acknowledge them as they see fit.

The alarm system is a vital tool for managing process control plants and monitoring operational integrity and it is essential that operators are trained, confident and well-rehearsed in the required actions to take in the event of an alarm activating.

The CSB investigation into the explosion and fire at the BP Texas City refinery in 2005 found that control board operator positions were downsized, and workloads were increased. Four open process safety co-ordinator positions for the ISOM and other area process units were not filled prior to the incident.

Operator fatigue and a lack of effective training and supervision were all cited in earlier CSB preliminary findings describing the root causes of the unsafe start up on March 23. Alarms were either not recognised or prioritised below others; eventually leading to the blowdown drum filling with hot petroleum spirit, overflowing and causing the Unconfined Vapour Cloud Explosion.

Operators

Having competent and well-rested operators, responding to alarms in a measured and controlled manner is crucial to safe and productive operations and should reduce unplanned downtime, increase levels of process safety, improve operator effectiveness and produce better process performance.

Safe start-up and shut-down

1. Types of start-up and shut-down - planned, unplanned, emergency, staged and delayed

A process plant is at its most vulnerable during shut-down and start-up operations. Several of the 'safety' controls may be ineffective or switched off to allow deviations from normal operations to occur or to quickly bring the plant up to normal operating conditions.

It is common to distinguish between different types of start-up or shut-down.

Planned

This is normal operation where start-up or shut-down follow a pre-determined sequence to bring the plant up to operating conditions and shut it down safely.

Planned shut-down is sometimes referred to as a 'turnaround shut-down'. It applies when the plant is closed for periodical maintenance and replacements. Such a shut-down is planned well in advance, often many months, as it is linked to both product supply (and hence income generation) and the assessment of plant requirements, eg life expired catalysts requiring replacement, development of fouling in key process areas, life cycle of equipment parts such as pumps, compressors, valves, filters,

In modern plant, particularly continuous operation process, the need to effect a full turnaround shut-down is reduced by the provision of sufficient redundancy in key process elements and plant design that allows for by-pass (partial shut-down) without overtly affecting production.

The shut-down operation will include a risk assessment(s) of the various shut-down activities and include the in-house and contracted workers to ensure all risks are made fully explicit and are communicated. Such a shut-down will be carried out in a controlled manner utilising knowledge and experience of the process and the various interactions which may occur.

Unplanned

This is where shut-down is unexpected, eg from an equipment malfunction (often due to neglect of maintenance), power failure, operator error, or similar unexpected event.

Unplanned shut-down may be partial or complete. In any event, this can be a dangerous period as the absence of any 'plan' for such eventualities requires close attention to the

detail of the shut-down to ensure the plant remains safe. The reason for and the nature of the required shut-down will have a direct impact on the issues to be addressed. More frequently, the unplanned shut-down involves only part of a plant. However, this may also increase risk as it is important to ensure that there is no onward or unexpected/uncontrollable impact on other parts for the plant and processes. For example, shutting down steam supply because of a significant boiler leak will impact on all steam-dependent processes if steam capacity cannot be maintained through redundancy or over capacity built into the system. In some situations, it may be impossible to know what stage a process reaction has reached. The result of shut-down could impact on product quality, involving, at best, loss to the waste stream (which may have inherent safety issues, eg flammable volatiles contained in liquid stream), poisoning of catalyst to sudden, even catastrophic release if the event has not been foreseen in the control procedures resulting from the Process Hazard Analysis (PHA).

Whenever shut-downs are planned, especially when partial, it is vitally important to ensure that the shutting down of one part of a process or support system (such as cooling water, power and other utilities) does not have safety implications for other parts of the system that may still be operating or idle in a 'live' mode, eg holding materials under pressure or temperature. So, it is important to carry out an adequate assessment of the risks involved. This holds true in circumstances where part of the plant or process is being shut down for repair, maintenance or alterations or where contractors are being employed who are normally unfamiliar with plant or process. A procedure should be in place to determine the compatibility, interference and limitations that the shut-down might involve or give rise to, particularly the interfaces between the plant shutting down and other areas and processes. This will usually involve a combined meeting of all interested parties (engineers, process operators, supervisors contractors, etc) who have prepared detailed descriptions and plans of what they intend to do and what impact there may be. Turning off a shared service, such as cooling water, steam supply, etc may well have a significant impact on areas and operations that use the same water, etc. Detailed risk assessments therefore need to be carried out to ensure the interface(s) between the various aspects and operations are understood and controlled through detailed and adequate planning of all aspects of the work involved so that they do not pose a risk to safety (or operations). This needs to be communicated to all those working on the various involved parts of the process and plant, and procedures put in place, including permit-to-work, where necessary, to avoid and control the risks.

Emergency

This is a specific type of unplanned shut-down that happens when a hazardous situation develops and action is taken (either manually or automatically) to shut the plant down. This is most likely to be the result of a situation where the safe operating envelope could potentially be breached. It may be signalled by local alarms, operator monitoring or external operating conditions such as adverse weather. When operator action is required, the importance of Human Factors (HF) will be paramount as operators need to make decisions and carry out actions without necessarily having complete information and experience. The emergency hardware and design of the Safety Critical Elements (SCE) as well as the emergency shut-down SOPs, should result in a controlled shut-down. An immediate review of the shut-down must be carried out to obtain knowledge about plant and process condition, and the reason for the emergency to inform future operations and guide the start-up after remedial work has been done.

When carrying out an emergency shut-down, the various stages will need to be followed where possible, but there may be extenuating circumstances, eg reactor cooling times, which mean that the shut-down will cause unknown deviations and which will require robust monitoring and attention to detail. Ideally, of course, the circumstances requiring an emergency shut-down would be foreseen, but this is not necessarily the case. Caution in emergency shut-down of any process is therefore well advised.

Staged

This is when the start-up or shut-down are done in stages. For example, some parts of large plant (such as catalytic cracking units) may not be quickly shut-down safely and may take several days to do so. In general terms, start-ups will be staged in the sense that there is a progressive implementation of the process according to both operational and safety requirements, eg inerting a vessel with N_2 before filling with volatiles to ensure no air-hydrocarbon interaction can take place, leading to fire or explosion.

All planned shut-downs will generally be staged to ensure that the progressive turning off of the process does not impact adversely on operations (eg fouling of elements, poisoning of

catalyst) and safety. For instance, in petrochemical plants, the last phase of a shut-down is usually the closing off of the flare stack as this is the last safety 'defence' where excess volatiles can be safely burnt off. If the flare is shut-down early, the volatiles will be directed to a more dangerous area or may not even be vented, leading to a serious risk of explosion or fire.

Delayed

A delayed shut-down invariably refers to a situation where an issue has been raised, eg leaking valve, but an assessment is made that the situation can be controlled until an appropriate full/partial shut-down can be dealt with. So, if a leaking valve is detected some two weeks before the planned shut-down, then, subject to assessment, it can be decided to monitor the leak and take local control actions until it can be addressed as part of the planned shut-down. This will inevitably lead to a higher risk and robust control measures will need to be in place.

At times, therefore, it would be advisable to operate a delayed or staged shut-down so that the implications can be thought through and controls put in place and monitoring of the shut-down instigated by competent workers.

Attention to detail and accurate assessment and planning of operations is thus essential (including pre-designed responses for emergency situations). It is also typical that during planned (ie normal) start-up and shut-down, there are more people engaged on the plant, including site workers and contractors. So, there is a greater likelihood of multiple injuries/fatalities, should something adverse occur.

2. Pre-start-up safety review

There are various stages prior to the start-up of a process:

- ensuring the plant is ready to operate. This can be a highly involved process in itself as it requires the checking and testing of all the physical and operational elements of the process before the plant is charged and the process initiated;

- typically, this involves a pre-start-up phase in which detailed checks are carried out to ensure that pipework, valve and other structural elements are correctly fitted and to the appropriate standard (design conformity);

- ensuring mechanical, electrical and instrument installations are correct;

Safe start-up and shut-down

- making sure equipment is 'run in' to ensure it operates as expected and to standard;

- and pipelines, vessels, reactors, etc have been properly flushed, cleaned and dried as appropriate.

The pre-start-up safety review is based on the Process Hazard Analysis (PHA) and its purpose is to identify design and other changes, including variations to maintenance and operational procedures. This should also include a check that appropriate standards have been adhered to, particularly for any Safety Critical Elements (SCEs).

KEY TERM

Process Hazard Analysis (PHA)

Many types of PHA exist. Their objective is to ensure that all requisite safety features are in place to deal with all foreseeable operational matters that could lead to the SOE being compromised. The PHA should always be reviewed as part of the MOC.

A set of start-up pre-actions will typically include:

- checking any modifications made meet any management of change requirements;

- mechanical preparation;

- chemical cleaning instructions;

- physical cleaning instructions;

- mechanical restoration;

- machinery run-in;

- tightness testing;

- pressure testing and gauge control setting;

- electrical testing/functional tests/energising;

- operation and calibration of alarms and relief valves;

- instruments calibration and functional test;

- loading of chemicals;

- loading of catalyst;

- heaters drying;

- chemicals boil out of steam generation facilities;

- verification of mechanical completion;

- communications (design team/maintenance team operators).

- testing and checking of safety and operational controls, including emergency blow-down, emergency shut-down valves, PRVs, trips and alarms;

- additional training given to operators (in cases where new plant or changes to existing).

All plugs and blinds should be checked. This may be removal of blinds set up as part of the shut-down or the fitting of blinds to isolate redundant sections.

All structural and physical connections should be checked by a physical walk through and direct observation.

Drainage, test and sampling points should be reinstated (to the operational function position), and vessels, reactors and pipelines checked for contents. It is vitally important to ensure that start-up does not commence unless it is verified that not only mechanical and structural elements are functioning, but that there is no hazardous contamination within the various components.

Where alterations, additions or variations to control parameters have taken place, they should be subject to the MOC procedures and process for the plant, and should include both hardware and software. The latter includes people competencies as well as computer software; the people competencies are underpinned by training and experience, coupled with supervision.

Any design changes should be fed into a PHA review to identify any 'ripple' effects that may occur upstream or downstream as a result for the change. This should be included in the MOC process, but is sometimes overlooked as not being considered important for reasons such as time and money, and because it is a like-for-like exchange.

Providing all is found to be satisfactory, the plant is then charged with process materials according to a pre-planned scheme that ensures proper process activation as well as safety. Then, feedstock/material is introduced to the plant and the process operated and adjusted to ensure optimised performance. Appropriate SOPs are utilised to ensure safety, eg inerting of vessels, pipelines, etc when introducing hydrocarbons (and other inflammables, eg dusts) to avoid the risk of fire/explosion if air is present. This will involve checking of emergency procedures and by-pass/shut-down functions and operability. These will include blowdown of materials from the process stream to a suitable end point, eg gases may be flared, liquids discharged to a holding/cleaning bin/collection vessel.

When operational settings have been adjusted and verified, then actual start-up will commence. That is the point at which the intent is to actually make product.

Alarms

In general, an alarm serves to assist the operator to identify abnormal, hazardous and unsafe plant and process conditions, identify faults and communicate them to maintenance, achieve optimum production and overall ensure safe and normal operations.

So, it is important that operators are able to identify, understand and appropriately respond to alarms. Actual positioning of alarms, whether in display panels or on plant/equipment, needs to be obvious and easy to see and read.

Another design aspect to be considered for an alarm is: does it require an operator response? The Engineering Equipment and Materials Users' Association (EEMUA), for example, recommends no more than six alarms per hour should actuate requiring an operator to respond. When this is achieved, the alarm needs to be prioritised so that the operator can respond accordingly. The alarm should only be presented to an operator if it requires a response. A good alarm system will provide the operator with guidance on a course of action to take to alleviate the alarm condition. This is especially important for high-emergency situations where the operator may be subject to an 'avalanche' of alarms as many parts of the process and plant register 'faults'. The operator needs, of course, to know what the appropriate response should be, but when the response is made, the alarm system should also provide feedback on the corrective actions taken, preferably on a supplementary display.

Another key feature is how the alarm is presented to the operator. For visual alarms, eg on a control display board, the positioning, colour and contrast of the alarm need to be designed so that the operator can immediately recognise the alarm in amongst all other displays. Likewise, the ambient light level of a control room will affect visual acuity as well as the possibility of eye strain. For audible alarms, it is vital that the alarm is not masked by the ambient noise level in the control room or location where the alarm needs to be responded to. Again, an audible alarm needs to have a distinctive sound, and modulating tone alarms (like warbling sounds) are perceived much better than single tones, but it is important to ensure that aural alarms can be easily recognised and distinguished from each other.

An electrician undertaking isolations in a switch room.
Getty Images

Safe start-up and shut-down

3. Plant shut-down

Important considerations for shut-down:

- all staff to be trained in the shut-down procedures;

- residual product/feedstock contained in pipework and vessels (both storage and reactors). It may be impossible to know precisely at what point a certain reaction has reached;

- residual temperature or pressure that needs to be neutralised;

- inerting and flushing of process components;

- the MOC implications (shut-down is a change and organisational elements may be compromised if the MOC does not include these, including such matters as authorisation, consultation and co-ordination, eg as between process engineers, operators, maintenance);

- SOP for isolation and quarantine of plant - small openings being plugged and larger pipework being blinded, etc;

- thorough checking and verification that the plant is in a safe state, supported by relevant SOPs including PTWs;

- where normal safety controls are compromised or turned off, eg venting, alarms, water supplies, SOPs and alternative controls must be in place;

- management of the SIS to ensure adverse signals interactions have been predicted and controlled (normal operation set up does not apply to shut-down; the SIS may need to be overridden, eg valve closing when low flow is detected, which in shut-down would affect the emptying of the plant). This includes oversight and focus on control rooms that should be fully staffed when shut-down/start-up takes place;

- communication through and with all stakeholders. Principally, these will be the operators and supervisors, the design team (who know how the whole process works and be aware of change history) and the maintenance team.

EXAMPLE

Case study

Here is a useful case study on shut-down periods using state-of-the-art methods for calibration and performance measuring, Online Detection of Shutdown Periods in Chemical Plants: A Case Study:

www.sciencedirect.com/science/article/pii/S1877050914011041

Safety critical performance standards

1. Reasons for performance standards for safety critical systems and items of equipment

In process safety, it is important to ensure that the various passive and active control measures, sometimes called 'barriers', are effective. At the design stage, it is important that standards are used to define how these control measures and Safety Critical Elements (SCE) should perform.

KEY TERM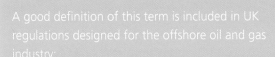

Safety-critical element (SCE)

A good definition of this term is included in UK regulations designed for the offshore oil and gas industry:

"Such parts of an installation and such of its plant (including computer programmes), or any part thereof-

1. the failure of which could cause or contribute substantially to; or

2. a purpose of which is to prevent, or limit the effect of,

a major accident."

Source: The Offshore Installations (Safety Case) Regulations 2005[2].

This is important as it sets the baseline for how the operational conditions should be established to maintain the process within the safe working envelope, and establishes performance standards (PS) against which the performance of the control can be monitored and measured. The oversight of the safety of the process can then be assured through inspection, testing and reference to the standards, eg as part of the management of change (MOC) procedures.

These performance standards should be established for all the safety-critical elements and for the equipment, including both individual items and grouped systems, eg emergency shut-down. Some of the elements may be derived from accepted external standards, eg fire protective coatings for structures and metal thickness for tanks. Others will be derived from an analysis of the design through the Process Hazard Analysis (PHA) and good engineering practice.

KEY TERMS

Performance standard (PS)

This is a general term used to mean an agreed standard that is set, and against which actual performance is measured and judged. Various models and methods are used for setting performance standards in process safety (eg 'FARSI' model).

Management of change (MOC)

In high-hazard industries, it is recognised that even seemingly small changes (eg to equipment, workforce, procedures, process conditions) can have large potential consequences if they are not thought through properly beforehand. MOC is a management control approach to make sure that proposed changes are properly assessed and authorised.

Process Hazard Analysis (PHA)

A systematic analysis of the hazards (and their potential causes and consequences) relevant to a particular process. This may use one or more specific techniques, such as HAZOP, What-if, FMEA (see later).

2. Relevance of the elements of 'FARSI'

KEY TERM

FARSI

A model for performance standards, which can be described in terms of its functionality, availability, reliability, survivability and interdependency (and usually abbreviated to 'FARSI').

FARSI is a concept taken from the offshore oil and gas industry as part of the means to describe the safety performance standards for plant and equipment, particularly in terms of what are known as safety-critical elements (SCE). That is, the parts (elements) of the safety control of a process such as **preventive** measures, eg strength of a container; **detection** measures, such as level gauges; **control** such as a remotely operated shutoff valve (ROSOV), etc, and measures that may prevent undesirable reactions or events escalating (eg pressure release) or **mitigating** measures, such as the emergency response of the system when they do.

Safety critical performance standards

KEY TERM

Remotely operated shutoff valve (ROSOV)

A shutoff valve whose operation can be controlled from a point which is remote (ie some distance away) from the valve itself, such as in a control room. ROSOVs are mainly used for rapid emergency isolation of vessels, pipelines, etc during emergencies, such as major leaks.

Additional reference source: *Remotely Operated Shut off Valves, HSG244 www.hse.gov.uk/pUbns/priced/hsg244. pdf*[3]

Functionality

This relates to the task that any particular element is intended to perform, so for example for a storage tank, the design pressure will be affected if the material of the tank degrades. So, to ensure integrity of the tank, there will be a standard for the degree of corrosion that can be tolerated. For an active system, such as a fire drenching system, the function can be described in terms of rate of discharge of the fire quenching media (eg water). The SCE is thus defined by what it is supposed to do, to what standard it is to perform and how that can be measured.

Availability

This describes and defines the time for which the SCE will actually be operational or available to be operational. For example, a pump required to remove material in a shut-down will only work if the power supply to it is maintained. Ideally, a safety-related function should be available 100% of the time, but there is always a possibility that a power failure might occur. This will need to be considered in the safety assessment and redundancy built in to ensure the power supply is always maintained. There is a close relationship in many cases between the Availability and Reliability (as described in the next paragraph) aspects of FARSI. Quantified risk assessment may be used to determine the downtime for any component and set a design target for it, for example 99% of the time (it will be operational) but in operational terms if the function is required during the 1% of the time the function is down then the system needs to be robust enough so that safety is not compromised. In the example given for the pump, if an uninterrupted power supply (UPS) is provided, this may also need a 'back-up' to ensure the safety critical pump remains operational should the UPS itself fail.

KEY TERM

Uninterruptible power supply (UPS)

In simple terms, a UPS is a temporary back-up power supply. It is installed between the incoming mains power and the critical equipment that requires a constant source of power (or requires power to always be available), such as process controllers, monitoring equipment, alarms and automatic shut down devices. UPSs are usually battery-powered and, should the mains power fail, the UPS takes over straight away, supplying power for a limited period (depending on battery life). The UPS may also send an alert or sound an alarm to alert workers to the power outage so that appropriate action can be taken (such as bringing a separate power generator online or executing a controlled shut down).

Reliability

This is often expressed in terms of the probability of failure on demand (PFD).

KEY TERM

Probability of failure on demand (PFD)

This is the probability that a component will fail to perform its safety function at the time it is needed. Note that a component may have more than one safety function/mode of operation and the PFD may be different for each of these functions.

For a safety-critical function to work, it needs to be reliable. When the function is required, it has to work; failure of the function creates a real risk of the process going out of control. All active systems (controls, valves, switches, pumps, etc) can be assigned a target value for reliability, providing sufficient operational data has been collected and collated. For example, a valve should be 93% reliable over a given operational period. This data will provide information by which to assess the PFD at the design stage and provides a means of describing appropriate maintenance and inspection schedules. Another way of doing this is to calculate the mean time between failure (MTBF) of a control element. Where a safety instrumented system (SIS) is in place, the reliability will be set by describing the safety integrated level (SIL) for the control loop.

Reliability is not used for structural or passive controls, eg fire protection. There may also be a limit to how reliability can be assigned to certain emergency controls, such as deluge systems, as these will not be in continuous operation and, in such cases, it has to be assumed they will work on demand. This has important consequences for maintenance and checking. Where a functional element has been assigned a reliability target, it is possible to carry out functional testing at intervals to ensure the defined reliability is being met. When this cannot be achieved, then more robust and specific inspection is required and any failure on testing must be recorded and reported so that lessons can be learned.

Survivability

This describes the properties and characteristics of the SCE when and after it is exposed to an emergency situation, eg exposure to fire or to adverse weather conditions. A classic example of this is fire-resistant cabling for fire alarm and fire control systems that have to remain intact (for a designed length of time) when exposed to fire. An SCE that cannot survive an emergency, or at least function until the emergency is under control, will degrade the total safety of the installation. This is particularly apposite in an offshore environment where the integrity of the whole structure has to survive severe weather conditions. In an explosion, blast walls need to be effective, if not, the blast will do significantly more damage.

Interdependency or interactions

This means defining the other relevant SCEs and factors on which the SCE being examined relies. As in the example above, if the pump relies on a UPS, then this interaction or dependency needs to be identified. Similarly, if structural integrity is required to maintain a means of escape when there is a release and creation of an explosive atmosphere, then the structure needs to be able to withstand the impact of the explosion to protect the means of escape. Electrical systems may need to continue to operate without causing ignition.

By using the FARSI approach, it is possible to describe and check the performance standard for each of the SCEs and also the SCEs in relation to each other and their relative dependencies and interactions. So, it is a methodical way of describing and understanding the performance standards for the various SCEs and provides a reference for critical issues to address in MOC, testing, maintenance, repair and operational variation situations.

For safety critical equipment, the concept of 'FARSI' should be considered.
©*Crown Copyright, Health and Safety Executive*

Utilities

1. Use of steam within the processing industries

Steam is used in a variety of applications in industry. A major use for steam is as a source of heating. Heating falls into two major categories - that for direct or indirect heating of space, and that for use in processes. Steam for heating at positive pressure is used in food-processing factories, refineries and chemical plants. Saturated steam is used as the heating source for process fluid heat exchangers, reboilers, reactors, combustion air preheaters, and other types of heat transfer equipment.

It is also used for motive power to drive equipment such as turbines (typically superheated steam is used for this purpose) and also to move liquid and gas streams in piping and to separate vapour streams, eg in distillation towers.

Again, steam is used for cleaning in a variety of plant to remove build-up of materials.

The wetting power of steam is used in processes that require humidification or moistening of materials as part of the method of manufacturing where the heat from the steam and its wetness is useful, eg paper mills and production areas using pellets. Steam humidification is also used in space heating systems.

Injecting steam into fluids atomises the fluid and increases surface area. The use of steam in this way is often found with flare stacks and other burners where the greater surface area improves combustion efficiency and reduces emission of pollutants.

Steam may also be used to achieve sterilisation in processes where microbiological control is required, such as food and pharmaceuticals.

2. Properties of saturated and superheated steam

Saturated steam is produced at the boiling point of water, at atmospheric pressure this is equivalent to 100°C. Saturated steam can also be created under pressure and the boiling point increases with the rise in pressure so it's possible to have saturated steam above 100°C. This makes steam particularly useful where heat transfer properties are required. Unlike hot water - which releases its heat slowly across a barrier - steam releases its heat immediately and so heating efficiency is increased considerably.

One of the problems with saturated steam is that it is still wet, as not all of the water is necessarily converted to steam (between 3 and 5% of water may be entrained in the steam). As a result, condensate forms - basically, the hot water falling out of the vapour. This reduces heating efficiency and also can create problems for pipe work and reactor vessels. The condensate has to be removed as near to the point of use as possible by steam traps. Saturated steam is sometimes known as wet steam.

If saturated steam is heated further, it turns into superheated steam which is effectively a gas. This superheated steam has a temperature higher than its boiling point and is more suited to transfer long distances through pipework or driving equipment such as steam turbines.

Moreover superheated steam does not produce condensate when it meets air or surfaces, further enhancing its utility as a means of driving equipment such as turbines.

Superheated steam is an invisible gas and not readily detected by the naked eye.

A third type of steam, known as vacuum steam, is also used. This steam is created by reducing the operation pressure using a vacuum pump so the steam effectively is below 100°C. With sophisticated controls, vacuum steam is useful where precise temperature control is required. This is achieved by altering the pressure.

ACTIVITY

Watch a video on superheated steam.

There is an example at:

https://www.youtube.com/watch?v=14RvYbYIlmY

Distillation columns.
Getty Images

3. Steam hazards and associated controls

Using steam in the process industries presents a number of hazards.

Thermal expansion

One of these has to do directly with the properties of the steam itself, that is, heat - particularly, superheated steam. Introducing steam into a pipeline or vessel exposes the structure to high temperature, which results in the material expanding. So, it is essential that pipelines and vessels are designed to take account of the expansion caused by the thermal heating effects of steam.

This is most usually achieved by building in flexibility using expansion joints or expanding sections that compensate for the thermal movement, as well as bellows and other design features to allow the material to expand without causing a rupture.

Prevention of the formation of vacuums

When steam gives up its heat in certain conditions (subject to pressure regulation), the steam may produce condensate (wet steam). Steam as vapour or gas occupies a much larger volume than water at the same temperature so that, when the steam's volume is reduced, a natural vacuum will form unless provision is made to allow for the loss of volume. In practical situations, steam input is controlled by valves. When the valve closes (eg on a heating coil), a vacuum can very quickly develop unless the pressure is equalised. It is therefore usual to fit vacuum breakers in steam lines to allow for the equalisation of pressure, preventing the vacuum. This is also important to ensure there is sufficient pressure within the system to allow the condensate to be discharged.

Water in steam lines (water hammer)

Water hammer results from water in a pipeline striking a fixed object under high pressure. This may occur during start-up or during variable conditions. The water in a steam system is accelerated either by steam under pressure or as a result of a low pressure void into which the water is 'sucked'. The water is abruptly stopped when it meets a fixture such as a valve, fitting, a bend or tee in the pipeline. The water then loses its kinetic energy as it strikes the object, setting up vibrations caused by the pressure shock that is imparted.

There are two basic mechanisms for creating water hammer.

One involves water entrained in steam being rapidly moved through the pipe (as condensate); the other is when the steam rapidly condenses, due to being surrounded by lower temperature condensate that causes the steam to rapidly condense to liquid. This causes a massive change in pressure due to the loss of volume, the result of which is that the cooler condensate rushes in to fill the void created.

The pressure changes in water hammer may lead to pipe fracture and, consequently, loss of contents. More mild cases of water hammer may be heard as knocking (hammer) or seen as movement of pipework. The pressure produced in the second type of water hammer, when the steam rapidly forms liquid, can (subject to pressure and temperature) result in massive damage to all pipeline components.

The first control for water hammer is good design of pipework and process controls. It also calls for the removal of condensate, improving the quality of the steam (minimise water), steam velocity and flow, ensuring that pipework insulation is maintained and removing the opportunity for cold areas to allow condensate to form (eg sagging in pipelines), controlling pressure and avoiding pressure drops, absolutely avoiding the risk of explosion by not mixing hot and cold (high pressure steam with 'cooled' condensate), ensuring steam pressure and temperature are reached before allowing steam flow, and maintaining steam traps and drainage.

Special care needs to be taken during start-up and shut-down, eg steam traps may not be functioning and water carry-over into the system is likely.

700mm cast iron water pipe broken by water hammer.
©Crown Copyright, Health and Safety Executive

Utilities

4. Water hazards and associated controls

Water is used extensively in the process industries for a wide variety of purposes. This section deals briefly with those water hazards that directly affect or have a bearing on process safety. So, only selected issues will be discussed.

Water exists in several states, depending on temperature. These states are solid, as ice, liquid, vapour and gas, as superheated steam. In the process industries, water as a liquid (apart from its incorporation into product) is mostly used for cleaning, testing purposes and also for cooling.

Vacuum formation during draining operations

In many situations, when tanks (and other storage vessels) are being filled or drained, precautions need to be in place to avoid the formation of a vacuum. If the filling or emptying rate is not consistent with pressure, equalisation across the vessel structure (internal to external) there is a very real risk of a vacuum forming (usually a partial vacuum). This vacuum then exposes the tank/vessel to pressures greater than its design loading. As a result, the structure will deform and may collapse. There have been many instances of this, including during testing and cleaning regimes. Vacuum breaker valves can be fitted so that the loss of pressure in the head space above the liquid is compensated when the tank is being emptied.

Another serious factor to take into account when using liquid water in systems that are primarily designed for steam or gases, is that it is much more dense. So, a pipeline usually used for gaseous products, if subjected to liquid water (hydrostatic) testing, may not be strong enough, or be on suitably strong supports to withstand the weight of the water. As a consequence, there is a risk of structural collapse if the pipeline and its supports are overloaded when filled with water.

When water is used, for whatever purpose, it is important to consider the chemical properties of the water, particularly, if corrosion might occur. The chloride, calcium and other impurities or additives in the water will need to be checked to ensure the water is suitable for the plant it is being used on.

Hydrostatic testing/weight

A typical use of water is for hydrostatic testing. This is a means of checking the integrity of the plant before start-up or after alterations/maintenance as part of the MOC procedure. Hydrostatic testing is often required as a final proof test after repairs are completed and before equipment is returned to service. While it will show whether leaks are present or not, the hydrostatic test does not, itself, ensure the integrity of the component beyond the time period testing. The pipework or vessel is sealed off and water pumped in to test that the structure can withstand the operational pressure that it has been designed to work at. Mostly, the pressurisation is taken to 150% of the designed operational pressure. The test is carried out gradually so that pressure is increased incrementally. Full observations and checks are made for any leaks and the test is maintained until the test vessel/pipe is proved intact. Depending on what the test vessel/pipe is to be filled with, precautions may need to be in place to ensure that the water is removed and the tested structure thoroughly dried. Testing will also require an operational procedure to ensure venting, draining and removal of hazardous conditions are carried out.

Vessels may also be tested by the expansion method. In this test, the vessel is filled with water and then further water is added and pressurised up to the test pressure. By measuring and calculating the weight of water retained and expelled when the pressure is released, it is possible to determine the degree by which the vessel itself expanded.

EXAMPLE

Case Study Example 1

Vacuum formation during draining operations.

In one example (cited in Sanders, R., 1993, *Chemical Process Safety - Learning from Case Histories*, 3rd Edn., 62-64, Elsevier, ISBN 0-7506-7749-X) water was being drained from a 25 metre high distillation column (the column had been unintentionally flooded due to a leaking valve). The draining rate was too fast, a vacuum was formed which collapsed the lower sections of the column, causing it to fall over.

Cooling towers - legionella and water-fog

One commonly found contaminant of water is that of the legionella pneumophila bacteria. These bacteria are ubiquitous in the environment and will colonise and proliferate in water systems that are not well controlled. The main risk is that water droplets containing the bacteria will be released into the atmosphere and inhaled, causing serious and life-threatening pneumonia. Anywhere water is used has the risk of providing an environment where legionellae can survive, particularly when water temperatures are in the range of over 20°C and under 55°C. The ideal growth temperature for the bacteria is 37°C (the human body temperature and hence the risk). As well as causing pneumonia, the bacteria also can cause a fever (Pontiac fever), which is generally less serious.

Legionellae live in two states within water systems. The first is in the planktonic state, which means that the bacteria are floating around in the water. The second is sessile, where the bacteria colonise the pipework and fittings. They do this by growing what is known as biofilm, a film that develops on pipework and fittings as the cells combine together and adhere to the surface; very often mixed in with the metal and other elements which form on the surface such as rust and corrosion, that in turn provide nutrients that the bacteria can live on. Once formed, a biofilm can be very difficult to remove. The main risk from legionella is where the water forms

droplets that can be inhaled. These are very small, around 5μ (5 millionths of a metre), and are formed wherever water is allowed to mix with air, usually by dropping. This is exactly what happens in a cooling tower where water from a plant cooling system is dropped through a forced current of air to extract the heat from it. That heat has been absorbed by the cooling process and needs to be removed so the water can be recycled into the system to undertake further cooling in the process. So, a cooling tower is an ideal breeding ground for legionella; the water is warm, the droplet size is small and there is always some carry-over of the water droplets out of the tower itself - simply because of the existence of forced air currents.

Extreme care must therefore be taken to ensure that the bacteria do not grow within the cooling tower water. This can be achieved by treating the water with a biocide, removing nutrients from the water, controlling temperature in make-up water and in ponds. An additional control is to prevent the spread of escaping water droplets by fitting drift eliminators. These are fitted in the top (or side) of the tower and force the water that has been forced out to fall back into the tower.

The inhalable droplets are not visible to the naked eye due to their very small size, so there is a risk to plant operatives and the wider community if legionella is present, as it is not always possible to know that you are breathing in the contaminated water droplets. This is the same situation when taking a shower or even running a bath - water droplets form but you are unaware you are breathing them in. A risk also exists wherever sparge pipes are used in plant and process systems to create sprays or mists. This includes fire-fighting and deluge systems; the risk is lower if the water temperatures are outside the legionella growth region. This may not be the case in hot weather.

Cooling towers.
©*Crown Copyright, Health and Safety Executive*

5. Characteristics and industrial uses of inert gases and associated hazards

Inert gases are of two types. The first are what are known as the noble gases, a small group of gases of which common examples are helium, neon and argon, which exist as individual atoms. In addition, other gases are also regarded as inert, typically nitrogen (N_2) and carbon dioxide (CO_2). They are called inert as they are generally unreactive and do not combine with other elements (except on rare occasions). They are sometimes used together in a mixture. These gases are colourless and odourless. This lack of reactivity means they are highly suitable for use in applications where oxygen or air needs to be excluded, and so they form very good fire and explosion suppressants. Nitrogen and argon are already available in natural air and are relatively inexpensive to purify and manufacture. Carbon dioxide is likewise readily available. These three gases therefore tend to be the ones used in process plants.

Typical uses include:

- inerting equipment to prevent flammable atmospheres;

- preparing equipment for maintenance by purging out hydrocarbons;

- removing air/oxygen in equipment before start-up;

- blanketing tanks to prevent the ingress of air to avoid flammable atmospheres in the headspace;

- pressure control blanketing - nitrogen introduced into the tank headspace to maintain a set pressure;

- certain welding operations;

- decommissioning equipment to prevent the 'rusting' process; and

- instrument air backup.

Nitrogen is also used as a liquid for cooling purposes and is stored in large quantities in liquid form.

Inerting

When inerting pipework and vessels, the gas is forced into the area and air is forced out. It is important to ensure that all the air is removed and that any overspill of the inerting gas is controlled. During the process, an assessment should be made of the likelihood of any electrostatic effects that might compromise the area, as fluids are removed or gases discharged. The purging prevents any fire or explosive atmosphere from forming by removing air (oxygen) in the system.

During certain reaction processes, an inerting gas will be used to displace oxygen and create a non-explosive atmosphere so that the reaction may take place safely in the reaction vessel.

During maintenance, purging will also be used to remove flammable material and ensure oxygen/flammable mixtures do not arise.

Hazards

Because they displace oxygen in the air, the inert gases are particularly hazardous in areas where people may be exposed to them. They act as asphyxiants by reducing, or completely removing, the oxygen from the air people in the close vicinity are breathing. This very quickly leads to disorientation, dizziness, and ultimately death as the level of oxygen reduces. Additionally, nitrogen differentially replaces carbon dioxide that prevents the breathing reflex (carbon dioxide is required to stimulate the lungs to breathe). Care needs to be taken to ensure that the emission, escape or actual usage of inert gases do not lead to situations where workers may be exposed in the breathing atmosphere. Use of testing equipment and alarms to both identify the presence/high concentration of the inert gas and also the level of oxygen in the air are imperative.

Both gaseous nitrogen and carbon dioxide are liquid when compressed and have low temperatures (CO_2 - 20°C, N_2 - 210°C). Exposure to the liquid as it gasifies on release will result in significant and perhaps life-threatening burns, subject to the extent of exposure. Again, nitrogen and carbon dioxide storage vessels and pipework need to be well insulated to protect from the danger of direct contact with people, as well as to maintain temperature.

Blanketing of storage tanks

One of the dangers of filling tanks with flammable materials is that a flammable or explosive atmosphere may be created either as the tank is being filled (or emptied, air entering via vents) or simply because an oxygen-rich head space is left above the liquid in the tank. To overcome the risk of this, a layer of inert gas is placed over the liquid in the head space, ensuring that there is no flammable vapour/oxygen mixing. The addition of an inert gas into the head space is known as blanketing. Nitrogen is the more common gas used for this purpose and as the head space will vary, a pad-depad valve is used to adjust the amount of inert gas in the head space. As the head space gets bigger, the valve opens, introducing the inerting gas. When the head space gets smaller (as the tank is filled) the other part of the valve opens, allowing the inerting gas to return to its storage vessel.

Nitrogen can also be used for pressure control, where it is introduced into a tank headspace to maintain a set pressure; this is called pressure control blanketing.

Uses as a fire-fighting agent

Because the inert gases replace air and thereby oxygen, they can be used for fire-fighting. Typically, CO_2 is used for this purpose in domestic and office areas and on some plant. For major industrial use and for process plants, a mixture of gases may be preferred. A typical mixture is 52% nitrogen, 40% argon, 8% carbon dioxide. The gas extinguishes fire by replacing the oxygen and thereby removes part of the fire triangle effectively. Care needs to be exercised to ensure that the discharge of the fire-fighting media does not compromise life safety by exposing people to asphyxiating atmospheres.

Pipeline freezing operations

Liquid nitrogen is used in several process operations, including as a coolant because of its very low temperature and its ability to maintain temperatures far below the freezing point of water.

In maintenance, alterations and repair work, liquid nitrogen can be used to avoid having to empty pipelines. By injecting nitrogen in a blanket around a pipe, it is possible to freeze the contents of the pipe. It is a very cost effective and relatively easy way to maintain plant and production integrity. The use of pipe freezing can be applied to a variety of situations including:

- repair/replacement of defective valves;
- pipeline leaks;
- adding branch lines;
- new process pipework/equipment.

ACTIVITY

Watch a video on pipeline freezing operations.

An example can be viewed here:

https://www.youtube.com/watch?v=o9C-G6x2ALc

Nitrogen use as back up instrument air

In a majority of situations, valve and other control processes may be operated by either air (pneumatic) or electrical drive forces. In situations where air is used, it may be possible to replace the air with nitrogen: permanently or on an 'as needed' basis. One of the advantages of nitrogen is that it is dry and readily available if used elsewhere in the plant. Another advantage is that it will not support fire/explosion. So, in a number of situations, the pneumatic valve control may be operated by a nitrogen feed instead of an air feed. As in all circumstances when an inert gas is used, care must be taken to ensure that leakage of the nitrogen does not compromise safety of workers and pipework is protected. For example, routing of a nitrogen-fed control pipework to a control room may expose the operators to an oxygen-reduced atmosphere if there is a fugitive leak. Likewise, oxygen level detectors may be required in work areas to alert workers in the event of a nitrogen leak.

Electricity/static electricity

1. Principles of electricity: relationship between voltage, current and resistance

Basic circuitry for current to flow

Electricity in a very basic sense involves the flow of electrons, the negatively charged part of atoms, from one place to another through a conductor. When the two poles (or terminals) of a battery are connected to a metal wire (or other electrically conductive material) to make a 'circuit', it causes a current to flow. The current flows due to the movement of electrons through the wire, 'pushed' along by the voltage (also called the 'potential difference') between the two poles. You will have noticed that the poles of a battery are labelled as positive (+) and negative (-). By convention, current flows from positive to negative (but in fact the electrons flow in the opposite direction). The potential difference is measured in volts and the current is measured in amps.

When connected to a battery to make a circuit, some materials are better conductors of electricity than others (ie flow is easier through some materials than others). We describe this using the property 'resistance'. A good conductor has a low resistance, eg copper; a poor conductor has a high resistance and is known as an 'insulator', eg glass, plastics, dry wood, rubber.

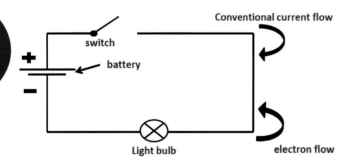

Voltage, Current and Resistance are related by the Ohm's law equation:

$$V = I \times R$$

Here V is the voltage (the potential difference), I is the current measured in amps (amperes) and R is the resistance measured in Ohms (Ω). Using this relationship, it is possible to work out a value of one of the elements if we know the other two. By adjusting any of these, the electrical supply can be modified to fit certain applications.

High resistance (R) gives rise to the production of heat as energy is expanded in trying to overcome the barrier to the flow of current.

There are two types of current, Direct Current (DC) and Alternating Current (AC). DC is current that flows in one direction with a constant voltage polarity (same difference between each end of the wire) while AC is current that changes direction periodically (in phases moving in both directions along the wire) along with its voltage polarity. DC is often the type of current used in short distance applications, eg batteries. For applications requiring greater power, AC is used as it operates effectively over much longer distances.

2. Hazards of electricity

Using electricity in process plants generally involves the application of low-resistant circuits at high voltage, except for heating applications. Using the V = IR equation, it can be seen that a high voltage with a low resistance requires a high current. High current is dangerous. There is a close relationship between voltage and current, and the impact depends on the conducting material. In terms of safety, the human body is generally a good conductor when earthed; ie the current can flow through the body to some other conductor. While current is mostly seen as the power that inflicts injury, it is important to realise that comparatively low voltages can cause injury. For example, voltages greater than 50V applied across dry unbroken human skin can cause heart fibrillation if they produce electric currents that pass through the chest. This has to do both with the V = IR relationship and also the length of exposure time.

The frequency of the current also has a bearing. Let us give some industrial context: in the UK, domestic voltage is of the order of 230/250 AC, in a three phase that rises to 440 volts; some processes will involve 690 AC and higher (supplies in some plants will be operating in kilovolts). The supply frequency is generally at 50Hz (Hertz).

It represents the number of times the current changes polarity; as the current is travelling as a wave through the conductor.

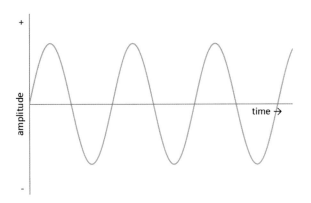

So the hazard of electricity depends on:

- amount of current flowing through the body;

- the frequency;

- path electricity takes through the body;

- length of time the body remains in the circuit.

Current in Milliamps	Effects
0.5-2	Threshold of perception.
2-10	Painful sensation.
10-25	Inability to let go, danger of asphyxiation.
25-80	Loss of consciousness from heart or respiratory failure.
80-2000	Burns at point of contact, death from ventricular fibrillation.
2000 and above	Cardiac arrest, burning of internal organs and tissues leading to death.

The amount of current will reflect both the source electricity as well as the part of the body that is impacted (comes into contact with it). Dry skin offers more resistance to a current than wet skin. If the current is sufficient, it will do damage. The impact of electricity on the body can involve localised surface burns, deep tissue burns and cardiac arrhythmia (the heart does not beat properly and blood is lost to the brain and vital organs). The nature of the damage will depend on the path that the current has taken through the body. As resistance builds up, energy is released in the form of heat. This may result in burns, so deep tissue burn damage may result and, in some cases, not be survivable, eg burns to the lungs. Surface burns may occur at the point of entry to, and exit from, the body. The frequency of the current may cause muscle spasm and result in the muscles 'freezing' so that, if the hand has touched a live conductor, the spasm will cause the hand to hold on and the person will be unable to let go. The heart and lungs may also be affected by spasm and stop altogether.

The longer the exposure, the greater the risk of serious injury. Longer exposures at even relatively low voltages can be just as dangerous as short exposures at higher voltages. Low voltage does not imply low hazard.

3. Electric arcs and sparks (ignition hazards)

An electric arc or flash occurs when two conductors are separated when carrying a charge. The break in the circuit can result in the current jumping from one conductor to the other, eg a switch mechanism or a short circuiting of a power supply line. Depending on the circumstances, current and voltage, the arcing can be extremely violent and result in the localised production of extreme heat and very bright light (a flash). Temperatures are generally very high - perhaps 20,000 to 30,000°C. The electricity continues to follow its path, and in doing so causes the intervening non-conducting material, usually air, to change properties, with the result that a massive current is produced. This can be seen when electric powered trains cross tracks and a brief flash of high-intensity light is emitted when the close connection between train and live rail is temporarily broken. If this happens in a process plant, there is an obvious risk both to workers in the vicinity and of ignition of any volatiles or dusts. Serious damage may also be caused to equipment and the power distribution system.

Electricity/static electricity

If a flash occurs, the instantaneous, significant/very large spark may ignite clothing and other material, or even an unexpected flammable atmosphere.

A useful form of arcing is that used in welding where the high-intensity heat created is able to melt metal.

Sparks caused are, in many respects, similar to an arc but involve much less power and limited ionisation of the surrounding air. Put simply, an arc is a very large spark, but definitions are unclear and vary.

Low-energy arcs can cause violent explosions in atmospheres that contain flammable gases, vapours, or combustible dusts.

Use of any electrical equipment in potentially flammable or explosive atmospheres can give rise to sparks. The designation of at-risk areas (eg where volatiles may be present) and the use of appropriate intrinsically safe equipment is mandatory.

Sparking also occurs with electrostatic discharge.

How arcing and sparks can occur during normal operations

Arcing and spark formation can occur in a variety of operational situations. Areas for concern are high-voltage switch rooms and panels when shut-down or start-up creates a gap across the switching, which may induce an arc if not correctly controlled. Defective or poorly wired cabling and connections may also give rise to arcing or sparking, as may operation of relays and incorrect use of tools or adopting incorrect procedures resulting in shorting or bypassing of safety controls. This is particularly so when systems are energised and maintenance or repair work is carried out live. Low-voltage systems may be at greater risk as the automatic circuit breaker may not be designed to act as fast as that on high-and very high-voltage installations. Failures in switches, not identified in preventive maintenance, can also cause a risk of arcing. Likewise, accumulation of dust and debris, especially in medium- and high-voltage systems in contact areas may result in arcing.

Condensation and corrosion may affect electrical systems and give rise to a possibility of shorting and sparks or arcing. Poor or faulty design and installation is also a risk. This latter can be addressed in the MOC and shut-down/start-up procedures.

4. How electrostatic charges are generated

Static electricity derives its name from the idea that the electricity is not moving. It results from a charge being built up on the surface of a non-conducting material, which is then dissipated by discharging it to a conducting material. Non-conductors give up or attract electrons relatively easily so that, when exposed to heat, pressure or friction, electrons will be released or absorbed. The material then becomes either negatively or positively charged, depending on whether it has absorbed or given up electrons. In this condition, the material now represents a potential difference to the surroundings, which then creates a potential for sparking to occur as the charge is dissipated. In an explosive or flammable atmosphere, the discharging spark may have sufficient energy to ignite it.

Static may be created by pressing two materials together. If the materials are of the right type then electrons are literally pulled from the surface of one, on to the other. A static charge is then created.

A more efficient method is to rub the two surfaces together, the result being that one loses electrons and the other gains them, so becoming positively and negatively charged. Although this is termed 'friction', it is actually the pulling of electrons from one material to another that creates the charge. It is friction at interfaces on a microscopic scale. This is known as 'tribocharging'. Applying heat to a material at one point causes the electrons to move and one surface becomes positively charged and the other negatively.

This has a number of applications in industry and is termed the 'pyroelectric effect'.

A special case of pressure causing a static charge is in the use of the 'piezoelectric effect' where stress applied to certain crystals creates a charge. This is commonly used in ignition devices for both domestic and industrial heating (eg gas hobs).

Another way of creating static is to place a charged material near to a conductor (or non-conductor) that allows its electrons to move freely. The charged material induces a charge in the originally uncharged material.

Many of these effects occur in process settings. They may occur between:

- liquid - liquid;

- solid - liquid;

- solid - solid;

- gas - liquid;

- gas - solid.

A number of different types of static are recognised. These are described mainly by the nature of the charging and the shape of materials involved. They include:

- **Spark discharges**

  These result where a non-conductive (insulated) material (eg plastic) comes into proximity with a charged material, which discharges across an air gap, heating the air to high enough temperatures to cause it to glow, eg a metal flange on a glass pipe (where the metal is insulated by the glass and is therefore non-conductive) or a person insulated from earth by shoes or carpet whose finger touches a charged object, such as a door knob. They occur between conductors that are not electrically connected.

- **Corona**

  Often found in high-voltage systems where a point electrode is created and sparking occurs as a result of the ions in the surrounding air being energised, eg in generators, transformers and capacitors.

- **Brush**

  Like a corona discharge but results from a blunt electrode and the discharge is therefore wider. Brush discharges may occur between an insulating material and a conductor or between two insulating materials.

- **Propagating brush**

  This results from thin insulating films in close contact with a conductor. The discharge happens at several points of the surface.

Conical pile (Maurer)

This happens when solid material (eg dust) is poured into a container forming a conical shape in the presence of charged air. The sliding of the material in the air causes a charge to develop which is then discharged via the top of the 'cone', eg filling of highly insulating bulk solids into silos and containers.

- **Streaming current charge**

  Another type of charge (a friction) develops in liquids in pipes. The surface of the liquid in touch with the surface of the pipe enables electron exchange to take place. As a result, the liquid picks up a charge, which is then moved through the pipe as the liquid flows, accumulating charge on the way. When the liquid is non-conducting (insulated), the charge is unable to dissipate back through the liquid and will discharge when coming into contact with air or another conductor.

TIG welding.
©*Crown Copyright, Health and Safety Executive*

The generation of electrostatic charge can occur in a variety of situations, for example:

- movement of conveyor belts (and gears) resulting in friction. A charge develops and will discharge from one surface to another;

- transport of materials. This generally refers to liquids and solids (as powders/dusts) being moved in pipes, chutes or being poured. It includes pneumatic transport of dusts and liquids in pipes;

Electricity/static electricity

- pouring solids and liquids into containers;

- sieving and grinding operations;

- agitation and stirring;

- creation of charge on workers walking in insulated shoes or on an insulated surface.

5. Control of electrostatic charges

Bonding and grounding

As spark discharges can only occur between materials that are not electrically connected the simple solution is to provide earthing (grounding), so that any charge is dissipated to earth. For fixed objects, this may be achieved by providing a permanent connection from the plant, structure, etc to earth. Moveable objects (such as filling bins) can be fitted with a 'flying' lead attached to the bin, which is then clipped on to an earthing connection at the point of use. The earthing lead needs to be robust and of sufficient size to allow for the anticipated charge. When connecting the earth cable, care must be taken to ensure a good connection is made, eg it is not covered in dust or debris.

In some circumstances, it may not be possible to directly earth materials. For example, liquids in glass-lined pipe or containers can be earthed by placing a tantalum plug in the line or by dipping an earth lead extended to the bottom of the container. This overcomes the non-conducting glass lining.

Brush discharges, as they arise from the use of insulating materials, can only be avoided by either not using such materials, which is often difficult, or by reducing the size of the surface.

6. Planning for power outages to provide emergency power

An essential issue for process plants is to maintain power. The majority of process industry activities rely on a constant supply of power. This is particularly important to maintain safety control functions. A power outage has the risk of exposing fail-safe systems, such as emergency shut-down (ESD), to failure. Additionally, a break in process activities, reactions, pumping of materials, etc due to a power outage, may well create a hazardous situation. It is therefore vitally important, from both a production and a safety perspective, that provision is made for power outages.

In plants that develop and deliver their own power, the same requirements exist as for plants that take their power from a national grid, although with obvious differences. Critical for this is an understanding of electrical power requirements, or 'loads'.

There are two approaches to consider:

- for short-time outages, up to an hour, an uninterruptible power supply (UPS) will be required to be properly sized and maintained. This may also be used to assist in allowing for power fluctuations;

- longer outages require provision of generators to provide a sustained power supply, often in tandem with the UPS.

KEY TERMS

Emergency shut-down (ESD)

This is a safety system designed to operate quickly to minimise consequences in the event of an emergency. The systems may rely on different types of devices to effect shut-down. An example is a remotely operated shut-off valve (ROSOV), described earlier in this element.

Uninterruptible power supply (UPS)

A UPS takes power (AC), stores it in a battery (DC) via a rectifier and then passes it back through an inverter (which restores the DC to AC) and back into the distribution system.

The provision of a UPS may be achieved in three ways:

- offline;

- online;

- line interactive.

The choice of approach depends on cost, requirements and functionality.

In simple terms, the offline system takes power from the mains and then stores it in a battery. It remains disconnected from the internal distribution system until there is a demand. Switching on can take 25 milliseconds, which may be significant for critical control functions. It is generally available for low-power situations (eg computers) operating below 1kVA.

The online approach is used where electrical isolation is necessary or for equipment that is sensitive to fluctuations in power supply. It is generally used for high-power applications. When the external power source fails, the inverter (which is permanently connected) drops out and power is continuously supplied. When external power is restored, the rectifier resumes charging the batteries.

The line interactive approach is an online approach that selectively taps off from the transformer under varying power conditions. This may result in small losses of power as the switchover is made. There is typically a two to four millisecond delay during the transfer from AC power to battery back-up power.

In general terms, UPS is self-limiting by the amount of energy that the batteries can store, so they are mostly only able to maintain power for a short period. Selection, sizing and monitoring of UPS performance is critical to ensure key process and safety controls are not impacted by UPS shortcomings or technical inefficiencies.

The precise use and application of UPS systems will reflect the critical risk control, SCE and functions within the plant and its associated processes, as well as SIS and type of operations (eg batch compared to continuous). This, in turn, will be reflected in shut-down procedures, should partial or full shut-down be required.

ACTIVITY

Watch the following videos on uninterruptible power supply (UPS).

https://www.youtube.com/watch?v=ZiPAKgk11hE

https://www.youtube.com/watch?v=S3gFqGfL3Tg

Use of generators

Generators, or more correctly, standby generators, are expensive to install and operate, but may be necessary if a long-power outage is going to affect production and process safety. Two types can be considered:

- portable;

- fixed.

Portable generators can be used before the UPS ceases to function. They must be matched to the power requirement of the equipment to which they are to be connected and a record

documented of the sizing, wattage and voltage ratings for each generator application. Generators may be kept on site or hired in. Safety procedures need to be in place to ensure safe connection and disconnection in energised systems.

Fixed generators can be installed to match the expected total load or partial required load of the plant. Depending on the type of system and connections, there will be a dead time between start of the outage and start-up of the generators. Power surges also need to be compensated for (eg by the use of voltage regulators; some types of inline UPS also 'clean' input power, as well as acting as a backup power supply when needed). A power surge may occur when the external supply is restored.

There are two critical aspects with generators:

- the first is to ensure that they are properly maintained and tested, and are fit for purpose when required in an emergency;

- second is to ensure that adequate fuel supplies are available to keep them operational. A fuel supply system that relies on an external supply may be vulnerable, particularly if it includes a reliance on electrical power (eg fuel pumps on a diesel system).

Dangerous substances

1. Physical states of dangerous substances

Materials used in the process industries come in many different forms, and during processing may also change physical states. There are three basic states in which substances can exist:

- gases;

- liquids; and

- solids.

Depending on the conditions, a substance can co-exist in more than one state, eg during melting, solid and liquid co-exist; during boiling, liquid and vapour/gas co-exist. Each state may be subdivided according to either their shape or hazardous properties.

Gases may be reactive or non-reactive. They may be heavier (denser) or lighter than air. A gas is defined as a state of matter, which at atmospheric pressure (at Standard Temperature and Pressure (STP)) exists in a form that has no defined shape or volume and will uniformly fill the shape of any container it is placed in. Gas particles may be single atoms, single molecules or a mixture, eg Ar, N_2, CO_2. Gases when pressurised form liquids.

Often called gases, but not strictly so, is the vapour that exists above a liquid. A vapour is not a state of matter but rather the result of the liquid and gaseous states coexisting at equilibrium at STP. In process safety terms, although there is a difference, it is often usual to refer to gas and vapours as being the same - they exhibit the same properties. Vapour usually results from boiling or evaporation.

Liquids are substances which, at STP, have a fixed volume but take the shape of the container they are in. They will create a vapour at certain temperatures, and when this occurs at STP, they are often termed as 'volatiles'. This indicates that above the liquid (open container or head space) the liquid is in its gaseous form.

Solids have both a fixed shape and size and retain their shape and volume; they do not flow. Solids may form large objects or exist as discrete small objects, such as dusts and powders. Each particle of a powder retains its shape, even though reference is made to 'free flowing' when it is poured, eg sugar.

Water is an example of a substance that changes its properties when temperature and pressure are raised or lowered from the STP. Water exists as gas (superheated steam), a liquid at STP and a solid when frozen as ice.

How these can determine risk potential

The form a substance takes will affect its potential to be hazardous. In the process industries, the main danger to be concerned with is that of fire and explosion. In addition, some substances have innate properties that make them particularly dangerous in other ways:

- **Gases**

  The non-reactive gases are usually known as 'inert gases' (cross-reference to inert). Reactive gases are classified by their flammability and by their chemical properties. Gases present two main dangers: one is concerned with their ability to ignite and/or cause explosions; the other with the danger impact on humans and materials. Humans because gases can be inhaled and be life-threatening, and materials because the gas may, for example, be corrosive.

  The particles in a gas are very thinly dispersed and as they will occupy any space, unless deliberately confined, they will disperse anywhere and everywhere, this includes vapours. They will freely mix with oxygen in the air and potentially form an explosive or flammable mixture (depending on the gas).

  Gases when released, especially in a confined area, will reduce the level of oxygen in the air. This may result in an atmosphere that will not support human life, eg a gas such as N_2 or CO_2 at sufficient concentration becomes an asphyxiant, posing a significant risk to workers, while other gases (eg ammonia and chlorine) will cause damage by burning the respiratory system. They may also cause damage to plant and equipment.

Liquids

These comprise a variety of substances in the process industries. Flammable liquids pose a risk of fire and explosion if an ignition source is available. As the liquid flows, the fire is also spread and carried to other areas of the plant with the risk of further damage and /or ignition of other materials. Typical liquids are fuels and solvents.

A number of chemicals in liquid form, such as acids and alkalis, pose a risk of damage to plant, environment and humans, depending on the nature of release and concentration. The advantage of such a release in comparison to gas is that a liquid can be captured by bunding and emergency containment, unlike gases that are hard to confine and generally impossible to capture (see fire control).

- **Solids**

The risk presented by solid materials depends on its shape, form and size. As a vapour does not form above a solid, they tend to be much less hazardous in terms of fire and explosion when of a large size. Smaller-sized solids, such as dusts and powders are, on the other hand, very likely to present a risk of fire and explosion if not well controlled, especially carbonaceous materials (those containing carbon). Some metals in a finely divided state are also highly dangerous, eg exposure of aluminium powder to water. The reason carbonaceous dusts are so vulnerable to fire and explosion is because, if they become mixed with air, they present a very large surface area creating a flammable atmosphere. In many operations involving powders, it is essential to mix them with some other reactant. In doing so, the powder becomes dispersed in air and may therefore become flammable or explosive. This risk can often be overcome by inerting the atmosphere in the mixing vessel. Likewise, operations such as filling from height, sieving and similar activities, create a dust cloud (and note also possibly an electrostatic charge) making them a potential risk for fire/explosion.

2. Meaning of terms

Explosive

The term 'explosive' indicates that a substance has the risk of exploding in the right mixture with oxygen (air) and if sufficient energy is available. Explosive substances have very low ignition energies. The energy may be created by heat, shock or electric charge (such as electrostatic friction). Some compounds, eg azides, acetylides, diazo, nitroso, haloamine, ozonides, are particularly sensitive to shock (and heat) and may be set off (explode) by touching the container they are stored in. Substances are categorised by the minimum energy required to ignite it and the concentration of oxygen (air) that will support the ignition and subsequent fire/explosion (see Element 4).

Oxidising

'Oxidising' describes the property of a substance to readily accept electrons from another substance. Its name is derived from the effect oxygen has when interacting with substances, so an oxidising agent can also mean a substance that gives oxygen to another substance. As oxygen is required for fire, the danger of oxidising agents is that they will easily 'oxidise' susceptible substances (eg metals, metal hydrides and organics) and create conditions for a fire to occur or make a fire worse. Commonly known oxidising agents are nitric acid, hypochlorites (halogen) and hydrogen peroxide.

EXAMPLE

Fire at Allied Colloids Ltd, Bradford, UK, 1992

One of the main causes of this incident was storage of incompatible chemicals together in the same area of a warehouse. Azodiisobutyronitrile (AZDN), a thermally unstable reducing agent was stored with a range of oxidising agents, including sodium persulphate (SPS), with which it can react violently. AZDN had been misclassified as an oxidising agent by Allied Colloids. The AZDN had also been stored close to a heater, which caused it to decompose. Some became mixed with the SPS, causing an explosion (some of which are thought to be dust explosions) and an intense fire, the extinguishing of which caused a great deal of environmental damage (from the fire water runoff into local rivers).
For more information see:
www.hse.gov.uk/comah/sragtech/casealliedcol92.htm
www.youtube.com/watch?v=G56UyZEL1A4

Dangerous substances

Flammable

'Flammable' describes the property of a substance (usually gas/liquid - actually the vapour above the liquid) to ignite when sufficient energy is applied in the form of heat. Under the Globally Harmonised System of classification (GHS), there are three categories for flammable liquids, based on flashpoint and initial boiling point. The flashpoint defines the lowest temperature at which ignition can occur when there is sufficient vapour released above the surface of the liquid. Obviously, if the ignition can occur at low temperatures, the substance is more dangerous than when it occurs at very high temperatures.

Safety of chemical reactions is a key subject for the chemical industry. In a chemical reaction, some hazardous materials are processed (mixed, stirred, heated, cooled, etc) to produce new materials. Usually, chemical reactions evolve significant amounts of heat (exothermic processes), being able to enter in irreversible runaway scenarios.

Flammable liquid category	Condition
1	Flashpoint < 23°C AND Initial boiling point ≤ 35°C
2	Flashpoint < 23°C AND Initial boiling point > 35°C
3	Flashpoint ≥ 23°C AND ≤ 60°C (ie flashpoint between 23°C and 60°C inclusive)

Storage of chemicals etc in warehouse.
©*Crown Copyright, Health and Safety Executive*

ELEMENT 1

ELEMENT 2

ELEMENT 3

ELEMENT 4

Reaction hazards

1. The effects of temperature, pressure and catalysts on rates of chemical reactions

In the process industries, chemical reactions are used in a variety of ways to produce new materials. Simply put, this involves taking raw material from storage, undertaking the reaction(s), isolating the product and preparing it for use.

The reactions may be undertaken in batch, semi-batch or continuous operations. The control of the reaction, both to ensure the correct product is made and to ensure safety, requires an understanding of the chemical reaction itself.

However, they are modified to allow reactant addition and/or product removal in time. A normal batch reactor is filled with reactants in a single stirred tank at time = 0 and the reaction proceeds. A semi-batch reactor, however, allows partial filling of reactants with the flexibility of adding more as time progresses.

Temperature

All chemical reactions involve energy to bring about the changes required. In the majority of cases, this energy is provided by raising the temperature. In simple terms, a chemical reaction results from the colliding together of the particles of two or more different chemicals. At low temperature, the particles do not have sufficient energy to react with each other and the number of collisions is low. As the temperature increases, more energy is imparted to the particles and eventually (at what is known as the 'activation energy'), there are sufficient highly energised particles to cause the reaction to take place. In very general terms, each rise of 10°C causes a doubling in the rate of reaction. This does not apply to all reactions, eg mixing an acid and an alkali is an instantaneous reaction that does not require energy in the form of heat to make it happen. But, for the most part, this applies to manufacturing processes. So, by adjusting temperature, it is possible to control the speed or rate of reaction.

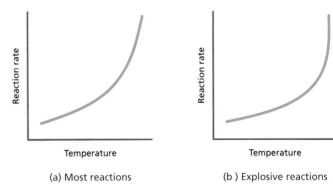

(a) Most reactions

(b) Explosive reactions

Pressure

Pressure has a similar effect to temperature. Whereas temperature increases the energy and therefore the frequency of collisions in a mixture, the application of pressure reduces the space (volume) between the particles and thereby increases the likelihood that collisions will occur. So, by controlling the pressure, it is possible to adjust the speed of the reaction. In many cases, a combination of temperature and pressure adjustment is used.

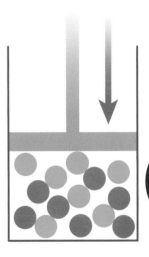

As pressure increases, the gas molecules can have more collisions

Reaction hazards

Catalysts

A catalyst is a medium put into a reaction vessel that changes the pathway (mechanism) of a reaction so that particles are forced into closer proximity. This increases the speed of a reaction by lowering the activation energy. Catalysts are not destroyed or changed during a reaction and are generally reusable, although they may suffer from poisoning by contamination with undesired trace substances in the reaction mixture.

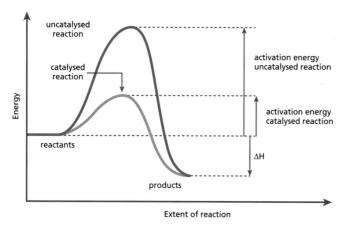

2. Meaning of terms

Exothermic reaction

The majority of chemical reactions give off energy when they take place. This is usually as heat (but may be light). Hence, the expression 'exothermic', to give off heat. Combustion (eg any fuel burning in air) is a common example of an exothermic reaction. Once it gets going, it generates a good deal of heat.

Endothermic reaction

An endothermic reaction, to take in heat, is the opposite. These reactions involve the absorption of heat from the surroundings. These are less commonly encountered but an example is the reaction between ethanoic acid (also known as 'acetic acid', the active ingredient of vinegar) and sodium carbonate (commonly called 'washing soda', as it is used in washing powder formulations). If you mix the two, you will notice the temperature of the resulting solution drops (it gets cold).

3. Thermal runaway reaction

Meaning

A thermal runaway (or thermal explosion) occurs when an exothermic reaction goes out of control. As the heat of the reaction increases, the removal of heat, to control the reaction, may not be fast enough to overcome the increased/accumulated heat caused by the reaction. When this situation is reached, the reaction will be operating (running) at faster and faster speeds as the heat it generates increases the temperature and hence, reaction rates. When the removal of heat is less than the generation of heat, the process will run away, ie go out of control. This mainly applies to batch processes as the quantity of unreacted material is much greater than that in semi-batch or continuous processes such that the likelihood of a runaway is greatly increased.

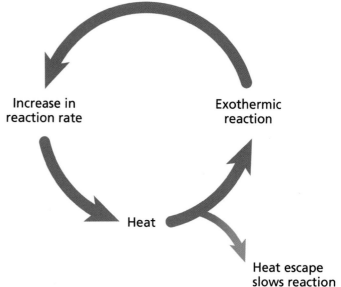

Process causes

There are a number of significant causes of runaway thermal reactions:

- incorrect charging, mixing incorrect volumes of reactants in the vessel, resulting in a reaction rate that cannot be controlled. This may also include a failure in the quality of raw material, thereby introducing unwanted contaminants that affect the chemical reaction. This includes inadvertent mischarging/addition of the wrong material into a vessel, causing an unwanted or unplanned chemical reaction;

- incorrect use of catalysts, which causes the reaction to go faster than predicted;

- failure to control the temperature, this can happen if cooling rates or cooling systems fail or are not operated;

- failure in the mixing, eg agitation/stirring not efficient, resulting in poor mixing and an imbalance in the equilibrium state;

- thermal runaway may be the indirect result of loss of power which, in turn, results in loss of the control system, agitation or cooling;

- maintenance failures, which mean that control processes are ineffective or compromised, eg leaks in cooling jackets;

- instrumentation failures, eg rise in temperature not detected and alarm does not operate;

- variations in operation, either as a result of the failure to apply MOC procedures, or a basic lack of understanding of the reaction chemistry;

- a design failure resulting in insufficient controls, such as heat cooling efficiency or provision of back-up facilities, eg alternative cooling water;

- insufficient operator training or familiarisation with the plant operations, resulting in several of the other causes; in particular, charging and failure to respond to alarms.

Additionally, a runaway may result from the inadvertent addition of compressed air, nitrogen, steam or other service fluids through connections into the vessel; this will increase pressure and promote the reaction to run faster. Likewise, exposure of the vessel to fire will increase the internal temperature that may lead to runaway.

ACUTE TOXICITY

GHS hazard pictogram – Acute toxicity.
©*Crown Copyright, Health and Safety Executive*

Reaction hazards

Possible consequences of occurrence

The consequences of a runaway reaction can be catastrophic. The least that can happen is that control measures result in the venting or dumping of product and materials out of the reaction vessel, perhaps in ways that have not been anticipated. This will rather depend on the type of relief systems that have been designed in. The result will be loss of production and probably damage to equipment.

In some cases, the rise in temperature may result in unintended chemical reactions, such as decomposition or even other runaway reactions.

The serious consequences include over-pressurisation of the vessel as a result of the reaction, which then ruptures the vessel and releases the contents into the surrounding area (Seveso). Depending on the energy of the explosion and the nature of the contents, the effect may be widespread.

As with the Seveso incident, where extremely toxic dioxin was released, there is no need for the vessel to rupture to cause disastrous consequences.

In reactions involving flammable materials, eg solvents, these will be released and may lead to fire and/or explosion which, depending on the situation, may cause localised or more widespread damage and injuries.

Likewise, serious and widespread damage may be inflicted if the contents are toxic or corrosive.

A catastrophic failure of the vessel may result in missiles (sections of plant and equipment) being ejected and causing injuries and damage. The worst case is the extensive loss of life to operators and the public and loss of the production facility.

4. Protective measures

There is a range of measures that can be applied to protect from thermal runaway. These measures may be preventive or mitigative. They include:

- containment within the reactor;
- crash cooling;
- drowning and quenching of reactor contents;
- emergency venting/dumping of reactants.

Containment

Containment requires the correct design and construction of the vessel so that it is able to withstand the pressure and temperature effects of a runaway reaction. This may not be possible for vapour-producing reactions as the pressure rise can be too great to be effectively resisted. The cost of building vessels with sufficiently thick walls may be prohibitive. To overcome this, the vessel can be encased in concrete or a steel/concrete bunker.

Containment is advantageous as there is no venting and the control is passive, requiring no intervention.

Crash cooling

Emergency or crash cooling involves the activation of additional cooling to the reactor. Sometimes, the term 'crash cooling' is also used to describe the addition of water (other cooling agent) to the reactor, which is more properly a form of quenching. Here, the term is used in the sense that some other cooling process is used. This might involve the use of cooling plant, such as a reflux condenser or an external heat exchanger. An alternative is to pump a refrigerant through the reactor coils or into the jacket.

The downside of these methods is that the temperature must not be allowed to fall below a level where the material will solidify as this may not only make the situation worse but also in all probability ruin the plant and equipment, requiring excessive clean up.

Drowning and quenching of reactor contents

Drowning involves supplying a significant volume of cold, non-reactive agent into the reactor - usually water (except in those situations where water may itself create an exothermic reaction, in which case an alternative is used). This may be achieved in the reactor vessel itself by having a gravity feed tank above the reactor that discharges into the reactor when a temperature-activated valve operates. Where space/volume does not permit, the contents of the reactor may be dumped into a tank of coolant, achieving the same effect.

In quenching, a non-reactive diluent may be added to the reactor (drowning is a type of quenching). Active quenching uses an agent, which itself can alter the reaction taking place by inhibiting the reaction. It needs to be carefully chosen so that all possible circumstances are accounted for, but provides a substitute for a direct acting inhibitor.

Similarly, an inhibitor (the opposite of a catalyst) may be added to reverse or impede the reaction by slowing it down, or stopping it. The use of inhibitors is complex; one of the problems is that adequate mixing is required and if the agitator is not working or the reaction is stratified the inhibitor will not interact effectively. Inhibitors are used in very small amounts to counteract the catalyst.

Emergency venting/dumping of reactants

Venting or dumping is another option. Most reactor vessels are fitted with a vent to release excess pressure. In a runaway reaction, these vents may not be sized to take the full over-pressure caused by the runaway reaction. The use of the emergency pressure relief may need to be supplemented and, in any event, the discharge should go via an emergency effluent handling or discharge system such as a vapour-liquid separator (knock-out drum). The pressure release device may also be a bursting disc. The pressure release is set at a predetermined level so that venting takes place before the runaway has become critical.

Dumping involves emptying the reactor and sending the contents for treatment.

Vented/dumped material may be treated in a number of ways, eg through a scrubber to separate out and recover materials, or flared off through a flare stack.

A vapour-liquid separator may also be referred to as a flare knock-out drum, flash drum, knock-out drum, knock-out pot, compressor suction drum or compressor inlet drum. When used to remove suspended water droplets from streams of air, a vapour-liquid separator is often called a demister.

Protective systems are rarely used on their own, and some preventive measures are usually included to limit the requirements on protective systems. It is not always possible to design a protective system to cope with the full consequences of a runaway reaction. The events of Seveso show this to be true. Hence, the importance of inherent safety being at the top of the hierarchy of process safety risk control (see Element 2).

An operator reads a gauge to check on pressure flow.
Getty images

Bulk storage operations

1. Hazards and risks

There are eight types of tanks used to store liquids:

- fixed-roof tanks (atmospheric tanks);

- external floating roof tanks;

- internal floating roof tanks;

- domed external floating roof tanks;

- horizontal tanks;

- pressure tanks;

- variable vapour space tanks;

- liquefied natural gas (LNG) tanks.

Overfilling

There have been a number of incidents where storage tanks have been overfilled with disastrous consequences. This illustrates that a very real risk is presented when filling tanks with hazardous material. Hazardous liquids may be present in a variety of process industries, including petrochemical (oil and gas), food processing (solvents) and drinks (ethanol). The immediate consequence is that the fluid overflows and escapes to an area, which it might possibly ignite and cause a major fire or explosion. The risk arises either because operators have no knowledge of the level in the tank, or there is an instrumentation failure in automatic filling systems. The liquid is released through the vents intended for vapour, or by over-pressurising the tank, which then ruptures. Similarly, the overfilling of vessels intended to separate gases from liquids results in the liquid entering the outlets designed to take the gas phase.

EXAMPLES

Explosion and Fire at the Buncefield Oil Storage Depot, Hemel Hempstead, UK, 2005

This incident involved explosions and fire at a major bulk fuel storage facility, starting when a fuel tank overflowed. The tank that overflowed had both a level gauge and an independent high-level shutdown, neither of which worked.

Explosion and Fire at Catano oil refinery, Bayamon, Puerto Rico, 2009

This is another example of tank overflow due to faulty tank fuel gauge, which lead to a fire.

Effects of vacuum

The majority of storage tanks used in the process industries are constructed of plate steel. They are designed to withstand the internal pressure exerted from the contents when filled. They are, however, weak when exposed to external pressure, so that when a tank is being emptied or draining, unless precautions are taken, a partial vacuum will be created in the interior of the tank and the tank will deform and, if the vacuum is sufficient, collapse. The pressure to create a vacuum is much less than that required to fill the tank. So, it is necessary to ensure that vacuum breaker valves are fitted so that the loss of pressure in the head space above the liquid is compensated when the tank is being emptied.

ACTIVITY

The following videos demonstrate what happens when a storage tank is not properly vented:

https://www.youtube.com/watch?v=2WJVHtF8GwI

https://www.youtube.com/watch?v=0N17tEW_WEU

Overloading of foundations

A fabricated tank is relatively light, compared to the loading exerted when it is filled with liquid, so the overall load up on the foundations can be considerable. If the ground on which it is built is soft or liable to movement, the loading on the foundations may cause them to become unstable with consequential damage to the tank itself and loss of contents.

Tanks may be built up on a solid concrete foundation or on to a circular ring beam foundation. The design of the tank, its construction and foundation has to be suitable for the intended contents. The density of liquids varies, and the weight exerted on the foundation and on the tank wall may be significantly different from product to product. Care should be taken to ensure that the tank design has been verified for the type of contents with which it may be filled so that the foundations are not overloaded. Deformation of the base may occur when the tank is filled and emptied and this may impact on the foundation itself, especially with high pressure tanks, when foundation anchor bolts should be fitted. Likewise, when the tank may be subjected to high wind sheering, it should be anchored by foundation bolts to prevent it being lifted up.

Failure modes for tank shells and associated pipework

The metals used for tanks and pipelines can be subject to a range of failure modes, eg creep, stress, thermal shock and brittle fracture:

- **Creep**

  Creep describes the gradual extension of material under a steady tensile stress over a long period of time, particularly in high-temperature conditions. Tensile refers to the pulling apart of the metal in a single plane. Another aspect is elasticity, which refers to the degree to which the material will return to its former length after stretching. Tensile strength and elasticity decrease with increasing temperature, which means that creep is more likely to occur at higher temperatures. Exposed to creep, the metal of a tank or pipe may deform and eventually fracture.

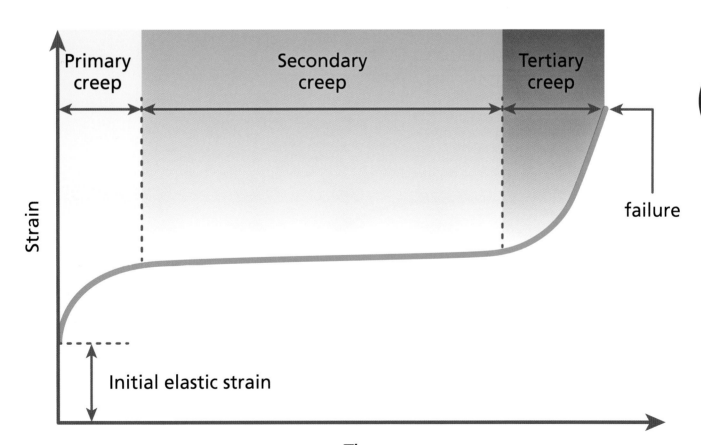

Bulk storage operations

- **Stress**

  Stress refers to the tensile or compressive loading placed on a material. Strain refers to the deformation that it will undergo when stress is applied to it. This gives rise to two broad categories of material; ductile, which will move under strain, and brittle, which simply breaks under strain. Steel is ductile and will yield before it breaks; cast iron is brittle and does not yield.

  Stress failures occur as a result of the impact on a material of the conditions to which it is exposed. So, in tanks and pipework, the metal will be subject to stress because of the loading exerted by the contents, changes in temperature and variations in loading. For example, a tank being emptied and then refilled will be subject to movement as the structure responds to the variation in the load placed on it. In pipework at flanges, openings and connections, there will be greater loading and therefore more stress.

  Stress corrosion is an example of failure that occurs when a metal corrodes as a result of exposure to a specific environment and is unable to take the load placed on it, eg mild steel exposed to nitrates.

  Similarly, in some situations, hydrogen atoms will invade steel and cause hydrogen embrittlement. At high temperature, hydrogen enters the steel and then reforms as hydrogen molecules, taking up space and putting pressure on the steel, which then cracks.

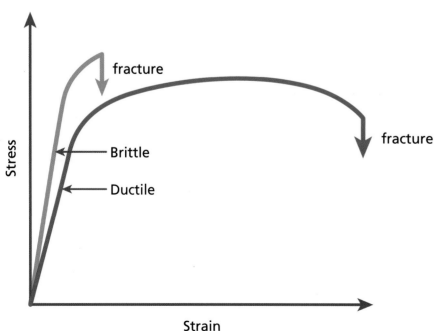

- **Thermal shock**

  Thermal shock results from exposing materials to rapid and extreme temperature changes. This causes the different parts of the material to expand by differing amounts, which in turn gives rise to uneven expansion. As a result, cracking occurs when the stress applied by the expansion exceeds the strength of the material. The crack will continue until the object or material fails.

- **Brittle fracture**

  Brittle fractures occur suddenly when the material is put under excessive stress and has no, or limited, elasticity. This may happen because the material is intrinsically brittle or the loading on it has happened so fast that it has not had time to be elastic. This is usually referred to as impact or 'snatch' loading. In brittle fracture, small cracks rapidly spread through the material, which then suddenly fails under stress. As there is no elastic component, if the two ends of a brittle fracture are put back together, they join up perfectly, unlike ductile fractures that have become deformed.

  Low temperatures can increase the occurrence of brittle fracture, eg materials used for storing and conveying LPG.

- **Fatigue failure**

  Fatigue is the formation of crack(s) as a result of repeated application of loads that individually do not create sufficient stress to cause failure. It may appear as thermal fatigue, contact fatigue, surface or pitting fatigue, subsurface cracking or subcase fatigue, and corrosion fatigue.

  The fatigue fracture is caused by the simultaneous action of:

  - cyclic stress, ie repeated actions creating stress, filling/emptying, loading/unloading;
  - tensile stress, ie putting a load on the material; and
  - plastic strain, ie the material does not yield (exhibit elasticity).

  All three need to be present to initiate and propagate fatigue cracking. Cyclic stress and plastic strain initiate the cracks while tensile stress is responsible for its initiation and propagation.

For storage tanks fatigue may also be induced by:

- wind load/vibration;
- pump-induced vibration;
- pedestrians walking on/over components.

Although we have discussed a number of different types of failure above, there are many other types. For example, corrosion is a significant issue, especially when vessels and pipelines are located in or near the sea, when corrosion rates can be significantly higher.

2. Siting of tanks

The location of storage tanks will be determined by a number of factors, including:

- size and type of tank;

- contents stored in tank (flammable, toxic, polluting);

- topography (level ground, sloping ground, high level, low level);

- purpose of tank in relation to process (feed stock or product, proximity to point of use);

- land use planning requirements (legal requirements for siting structures);

- total inventory (how much material is being stored); and

- whether the tank is to be underground, above ground or mounded.

These factors will be assessed together to determine the risk of loss of containment and the consequences on site and off site.

The principal risks are:

- fire;

- explosion;

- release of toxic substances (human impact);

- environmental damage.

Tanks will generally not be sited within 50 metres of a spring, well or borehole or 10 metres of a watercourse. Local drainage requirements should prevent spillage entering the drains, seeping into aquifers or polluting ground water. Loss of containment has involved fires where flammable liquids have travelled through drains and been ignited at remote locations.

Bulk storage operations

Where tank venting will result in local exposure because of man-made or natural topography, consideration should also be given to appropriate access for emergency vehicles and provision of fire-fighting, eg a water ring main and fixed monitors.

An assessment should be made of the consequences of a worst-case scenario involving a loss of containment and the various scenarios (including domino scenarios) that might cause that to happen. Consequences will include:

- injuries and fatalities on site and off site;

- damage on site and off site.

In the case of fire/explosion, the impact on people may involve a calculation of the thermal dose that would occur if a fire results from loss of containment. That will involve considering three situations:

- the first is where people may be engulfed by the fire;

- the second is where people may be affected by the thermal radiation from the fire (outside the fire);

- thirdly, the impact on people inside a building that is exposed to fire/radiation.

A similar assessment will be made of the likely overpressure that would be caused by an explosion.

Photograph showing how tanks can be spaced and sited.

Distance

Both these assessments will indicate typical safe distances for siting of storage tanks. This generally involves setting a separation distance between the tank and community areas so that in the event of fire/explosion, the consequences will be limited. Areas where operational workers are likely to be, may also be separated, but will take into account the practicality on a case-by-case basis. Although separation distances are useful, they are not an exact mitigation measure as blast overpressure may be significant, as was the case at Buncefield, and weather conditions will have an impact on the dispersion of vapour clouds.

Tanks above ground should be sited in a well-ventilated position separated from the site boundary, occupied buildings, sources of ignition and process areas. A minimum distance for large tanks from boundaries is generally regarded as 15m and between 10m and 15m between tanks, depending on the type of tank. These distances are notional and are simply designed to allow time for emergency procedures to get put into place. They will not prevent fire spread by heat radiation, should a fire develop.

ACTIVITY

Have a look at the following about general considerations for storage of these liquids in bulk.

Storage of flammable liquids in tanks, available from:

www.hse.gov.uk/pUbns/priced/hsg176.pdf

Property

On-site buildings can be protected by explosion walls and passive fire protection built into the structures. Again, calculation may be necessary to ensure that buildings are robust to withstand worst-case scenarios. Off-site buildings should be protected by sufficiently large separation distances, but as the Buncefield incident showed, this may not be realistic in practice.

Other tanks

Siting of tanks should also take into consideration the location of other storage vessels, particularly those with dangerous substances and the vulnerability of process lines. For example, co-locating oil storage tanks with chlorine tonners runs the risk of chlorine release if the tonner is involved in a fire or explosion. In general terms, the larger the tank, the greater the separation distances required, but note the minimum separation distance of 10m to 15m between fuel tanks is reduced to 3m. This also applies to tanks with identical contents as shown by the progressive oil tank fires at Milford Haven and, more recently, Buncefield.

Oil refinery plant and equipment.
©*Crown Copyright, Health and Safety Executive*

Ventilation

The majority of tanks will need to be ventilated to allow for the variation in internal and external pressure during filling and emptying. If the tank is venting to atmosphere, then the dispersion of any flammable volatiles and the air mixture needs to be controlled to ensure flammable/explosive mixtures are not produced and toxic vapours are not released. Tanks above ground should be sited in a well-ventilated, unobstructed position separated from the site boundary, occupied buildings, sources of ignition and process areas. This will ensure that any fugitive emissions, spillages, etc from tanks, transfer facilities, vent pipes, etc will be readily dispersed in the open air.

3. Filling of tanks

Since the Buncefield disaster, the filling of tanks, particularly hydrocarbon tanks, has received critical reassessment with a number of recommendations for improvement (for fuel storage operations). What is absolutely critical is that the system for filling a tank and associated risk reduction measures should be foolproof and have the required safety integrity level (SIL), so that there is certainty about how much liquid has gone into a tank and when it is filled to the required level (this will be a proportion of the maximum design level). Filling should be carried out at such a speed that the tank is able to equalise pressures by means of the designed venting arrangements. The operator should be competent in the filling system and understand the control procedures and equipment. Filling may be carried out remotely via pipeline or locally from a tanker. Following on from Buncefield, the receiving party should have control and authority over the filling operations and not the delivering party.

Overfilling

Continuous monitoring should be used when filling storage tanks to protect against overfilling. The volume of the receiving vessel and its content level should be known before filling commences.

Alarms

Tanks are generally fitted with two alarm trip systems. The first is the high level alarm (LAH), which indicates that the normal operational level for the tank has been exceeded. This alarm should not be used as the reference point for the filling operation. The second alarm is the high high level (LAHH), which references the maximum design capacity of the tank. If this level is exceeded, the tank will overpressurise and overflow, leading to loss of containment (LOC).

Tanker connections

The use of mobile road tankers, either delivering or loading, presents a different set of risks. The mobile nature of the operation means that a connection has to be made between the vehicle tank and the plant. This may be achieved either by using pumping equipment on the vehicle or the site's fixed pump. The latter has the advantage that the vehicle can be isolated for the operation by switching off the engine and ancillaries. The connection is made with a flexible hose, and the filling point should be provided with non-return valves or dry break couplings. Historically, a number of incidents have occurred when drivers drive off leaving the hose still coupled to the tanker or have failed to properly secure the vehicle when on sloping ground (leading to a runaway vehicle). This has been overcome by the provision of breakaway couplings which, if separated by force, close and prevent spillage. The two key risk areas for loading tankers are static and siphoning. This requires that the tanker and the filling point are earth-bonded, and the end of the tank filling line extends below the lowest normal operating level of the liquid, to avoid the generation of static electricity by splash filling. Likewise, dipping rods should be earthed.

Bulk storage operations

4. Floating roof tanks

There are a number of types of tanks used for storage. Of the vertical tanks, there are two basic types of floating roof - internal and external, and fixed roof or atmospheric tanks.

External roof

Floating roof tanks (both external and internal roof types) work on the principle that the roof floats on the top of the liquid inside the tank. The advantage of this is that there is no head space above the liquid and the formation of vapour is virtually eliminated. So, emissions to air are controlled. Such tanks are used for the more flammable liquids that have a high-vapour pressure, low flash point. The external (open to the elements) floating roof tank (EFRT) consists of an open-topped cylindrical steel shell equipped with a roof that floats on the surface of the stored liquid, rising and falling with the liquid level. The roof comprises a deck fittings and rim seal system that is designed to keep out rainwater and prevent vapour emissions. The roof is typically on a pontoon, although there are other variants. Beneath the deck are a series of legs that enable the roof to stand about 2m clear of the base when the tank is empty to enable internal maintenance and inspection work. This is referred to as 'landing' the roof.

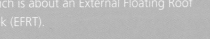

CASE STUDY

Have a look at the following Case Study which is about an External Floating Roof Tank (EFRT).

It can be viewed at:
http://www.sozogaku.com/fkd/en/cfen/CC1000167.html

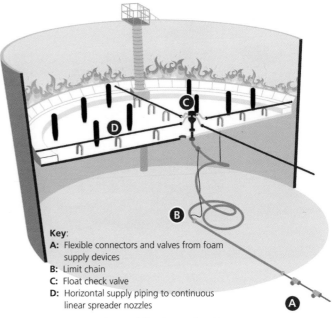

Key:
A: Flexible connectors and valves from foam supply devices
B: Limit chain
C: Float check valve
D: Horizontal supply piping to continuous linear spreader nozzles

External floating roof tank.

Internal roof

The Internal Floating Roof Tank (IFRT) operates like the external roof but has both a permanent fixed roof and a floating roof inside. There are two basic types of internal floating roof tanks:

- tanks in which the fixed roof is supported by vertical columns within the tank;

- tanks with a self-supporting fixed roof and no internal support columns.

These tanks may be purpose built or be converted from either an EFRT or fixed roof tank. A fixed roof is generally there to protect the tank contents from the environment, wind and rain. Within the space between the deck and the fixed roof, provision is made for circulation vents to allow natural ventilation of the vapour space, reducing the accumulation of product vapours and possible formation of a combustible mixture. A variant of the IFRT is the closed roof FRT that has a Pressure-Vacuum (PV) vent and may also use a gas blanketing system.

Landing the roof

When a FRT tank is being emptied, the roof is landed on its legs. The legs of a floating roof do not let the roof go below a certain height (1.5 - 2.0m) from bottom (local conditions). This is a relatively uncommon event, perhaps once in every 5 to 10 years (save for emergencies).

However, at this stage, the roof is no longer floating on the liquid, so as the tank is emptied, the space fills with vapour that has to be vented by an in-breather. When the tank is refilled, the opposite applies and an out-breather vent is required. During this period the tank becomes hazardous due to the presence of the vapour/air mixture. If the roof is landed because the level of liquid is below the landing level, then the emissions to atmosphere from tanks are greater and remain so until the tank is either completely emptied and purged of organics, or the tank is refilled and the roof is again floating. These emissions are known as 'landing loss emissions'.

Sinking the roof

EFRT are subject to the elements, and heavy rainfall can result in a water loading on the roof which, in conjunction with other issues, may result in the roof sinking into the content of the tank. The sinking may be a result of loss of buoyancy in the roof due to an imbalance in the supporting structure.

For example, water (such as from fire-fighting) may find its way into one of the pontoons, destabilising the roof deck, causing it to sink into the tank, leading to loss of containment.

In one case, fire-fighting water activated an ESD and one of

the pontoons filled with water, destabilising the roof deck that sank into condensate in the tank, leading to loss of containment.

Likewise, an incorrect design based on loading may result in the roof sinking if the weight of the roof is not supported by the liquid on which it is floating due to insufficient buoyancy.

Rim seal fires/failures

Floating roofs have around the edge a double seal that is designed to keep water out and vapour in. The seal may fail due to wear and tear, but is also subject to movements in the tank itself. Such movements can be caused by wind pressure, ground movement and internal pressure changes (filling/emptying). If the rim fails, then rainwater will enter and mix with the contents of the tank but, more importantly, the surface will be exposed to air, which may give rise to flammable or explosive mixtures.

One consequence of this is the risk of fire. A fire in the rim of a tank is generally covered by a fire protection system installed in the roof, eg foam discharge, and although not uncommon, is mostly readily resolved. Ignition comes from either a lightning strike or a localised induced static charge.

5. Fixed roof

Fixed-roof tanks comprise a cylindrical steel shell with a cone- or dome-shaped roof. The roof is permanently fixed (welded) to the tank shell. Modern fixed-roof storage tanks are fully welded and designed to be both liquid and vapour tight. Older tanks may be of a riveted or bolted construction and are not vapour tight. These tanks are used for low-vapour pressure, high-flash point liquids that are stable at atmospheric pressure. This means that there is minimum vapour release as the vapour and air are balanced. Variations in temperature caused by weather or by product charging at an elevated temperature will be vented through a pressure-vacuum valve. This limits the extent of venting and allows the tank to operate at a slight internal pressure or vacuum, which in turn minimises losses.

Pressure and vacuum hazards (ref. 3.4)

Pressure and vacuum hazards were introduced earlier in this element. Tanks, especially fixed-roof tanks, are susceptible to external pressure. While they may be overloaded by overpressurised filling, they are more likely to collapse if a vacuum forms internally when they are emptied.

Bulk storage operations

6. Bunding

In order to limit the consequences of loss of containment, tanks either individually or collectively, when they have the same contents, are surrounded by a bund wall. This is an impervious wall that is constructed, usually from concrete, that is designed to retain the contents of the tank(s) should there be a failure and the contents be released.

Volume and area sizing

The area contained by the bund wall and the volume that the area can contain should be no less than 110% of the total volume of the tank(s). The height of the wall is determined by the area that can be bunded and the volume the area needs to contain. The wall needs to be sufficiently far from the tank and high enough to ensure it is effective and can contain any boil over or top loss, which may well discharge like a fountain or spigot, as well as bottom loss, and likewise catastrophic failure where the contents will disperse like a tidal wave. The bund needs to be high enough to be effective in retaining the liquid but not so high that normal operations, inspection and maintenance, etc cannot be achieved.

Construction

The design and construction of the bund should allow for the collection of rainwater and its removal without compromising the retention capacity of the bund. It is usual to provide a drain-off point to remove water, which is suitably sealed and a sloping floor in the bund to promote drainage. The drain-off point will normally be manually operated and kept closed. It is important to keep the bund clear, otherwise the volume it can retain will be compromised. For the same reasons, it is important to inspect and maintain bunds regularly as, especially if outdoors, they are subject to deterioration from ageing, weathering, vegetation growth and direct physical damage (such as from vehicle impact). In large installations, the use of earth mounding may be employed as a means of retaining releases. For situations where the bund may be exposed to liquids stored above their boiling point, the wall can be treated with insulating material to assist in reducing the evaporation rate.

Valving arrangements

Where pipework and valves need to pass through the bund wall, it is important to ensure that an adequate (and resistant) seal is provided so that there can be no escape of content through the opening. Shut-off valves should be both inside and outside the bund, with shut-off valves in a line both within the bund and outside it. The inner shut-off should be as close to the tank as possible; non-return valves should also be fitted to filling lines. Isolating valves and ROSOVs should be fully functional and fail to safe. Lines for draining tanks and the valves should be blanked off.

7. Protection from extremes of weather

Tanks may need to be protected from extremes of weather. In both hot and cold climates, the tank will be exposed to wide variations in temperature. If this is assessed as an issue, the tank can be insulated. High wind loadings may also affect the tank by causing distortion and uplifting from the base. Distortion can be limited by girding the tank with metal bands. Trace heating may need to be provided on pipework for some materials.

8. Lightning strikes

A fairly significant risk for tanks is lightning strike. The power of such a strike can ignite volatiles and cause catastrophic failure. Lightning striking a tank can create a current that will induce sparking some distance from the strike point where touching points are not well bonded together. Puncture of the tank skin or formation of local hot spots will ignite flammable vapours. Welded fixed-roof tanks are not that susceptible to lightning strike but floating roof tanks are.

Control measures

Tanks should be protected by the placing of lightning conductors at the appropriate attachment points. Attachment refers to the location where lightning is more likely to hit (attach). For EFRTs, this point is the rim of the tank and also the roof when it is in a high position. Unfortunately, it has been shown that it is not easy or effective to bond the roof with the shell of the tank as there is a lack of continuity between the roof and the shell.

Control includes the use of inerting to keep the level of flammable vapours down and ventilation to reduce the hydrocarbons in the air.

9. Chemical warehousing

Storage of chemicals in the process industry, other than in bulk storage vessels, presents a number of risks, chiefly arising from the hazardous nature of the stored substances and the consequences arising from inadvertent mixing of incompatible chemicals, leaking and spillage from containers and possible reactions from exposure to elevated temperatures, including significant release of dust and powders and solvents.

Example of leaking bulk storage.
©*Crown Copyright, Health and Safety Executive*

Assessment and understanding of potential chemical hazards present

When chemicals are to be stored, a detailed assessment should be carried out to fully understand:

- the hazardous nature of the substance(s) to be stored, including its form (liquid, solid, powder, dust, etc), its physical properties (flammability, pH, etc) and relevant reaction chemistry information (eg reacts with water). This information should be obtained from the suppliers/ manufacturers' safety data sheets (SDS) (formerly MSDS). For substances created and stored on site (eg distribution warehousing or stock holding), a similar set of information should be produced;

- how the material will be transported, eg in bulk containers, metal drums, fibre drums, Intermediate Bulk Containers (IBCs), Flexible Intermediate Bulk Containers (FIBCs), etc This will also include the means of transportation, eg forklift truck;

- the inventory likely to be involved, volumes/weight stored at any one time;

- if there are any likely sources of ignition, including electrostatic or creation of flammable/explosive atmospheres;

- topography and how any spillage or release might impact on local areas. This will include the presence of drainage, watercourses and vulnerability of buildings;

- Temperature effects, eg some substances may degrade at higher temperature or become unstable (relative).

ACTIVITY

For more information on chemical warehousing, go to:

www.hse.gov.uk/pUbns/priced/hsg71.pdf

ACTIVITY

Refer back to the Allied Colloid Fire example discussed earlier. In relation to assessing potential chemical hazards, how could the incident have been avoided or mitigated?

Think about:

- the hazard categories of the substances involved;

- their compatibility and segregation arrangements;

- the quantities likely to be stored;

- sources of ignition or thermal decomposition (for thermally unstable compounds);

- the impact tackling the fire may have on the environment (pollution).

Siting, location and security

Once a firm understanding of the likely risks involved in the warehousing activities has been achieved, consideration can be given to where the warehouse should be sited, together with its construction (eg blast panels if there is an explosion risk). The local topography may indicate, for example, that the warehouse should be sited away from watercourses, at lower or higher level, depending on the assessment of risk. The relative proximity of community buildings, housing, schools, hospitals, etc will need to be factored into the siting of warehousing (or external storage), together with legal requirements for separation distances of specified materials, eg LPG cylinders.

Bulk storage operations

Also to be considered are the various routes to be used for receiving at and dispensing from the warehouse/storage areas. This includes the ability for vehicles to manoeuvre (eg risk of collision with stored materials or increased chance of spillage) and the availability of access for emergency vehicles including fire-fighting facilities, eg open water.

Storage areas need to be maintained secure. This includes both the prevention of trespasser activity and arson, as well as stock control. It is important to ensure that physical security is maintained so that entry through doors is only by authorised people and windows and other openings are kept secure, commensurate with fire safety requirements and maintenance activities. Security should not compromise fire safety and a balance sometimes has to be made between the two, eg high-level venting for fire control may provide a route of entry. Having good physical controls, eg lockable doors, coupled with authorisation, can successfully achieve the inadvertent incorrect storage of incompatible materials (eg in absence of the authorised warehouse workers, someone directs acids to be stored in the alkaline area).

Minimised inventories

A clear way to reduce the consequences of an untoward event, release, spillage, fire, etc is to reduce the total volume of material that is exposed at any one time. This may be easier said than done and will depend on production needs and available space. However, it may be achieved by separating storage so that the possibility of mass release is avoided. Just-in-time resupply will also facilitate minimisation of inventory as well as general stock management. Direct delivery to point of use can also be utilised to reduce inventory held on site.

Separation and segregation of dangerous goods

Where inventory needs to be kept on site, it is important to ensure that incompatible materials are stored separately to avoid inadvertent mixing and so to limit the possibility of chemical reactions leading to fire or explosion. For example, substances such as acids and alkalis should be stored separately from each other and segregated from all other materials. A detailed understanding of chemical and physical properties is therefore required to ensure that adverse reactions cannot occur.

Control of ignition sources

For volatiles, eg solvents and potentially explosive/flammable situations, it will be imperative that sources of ignition are identified and controlled. These include the more obvious sources, such as smoking on site, even in susceptible open areas and use of mobile phones and forklift trucks (build-up of static and charging of batteries, etc). Control over hot work and maintenance activities will also need to be included, to avoid ignition of susceptible materials. This includes both in normal storage and in release/spill situations.

Smoking shelter.
©*Crown Copyright, Health and Safety Executive*

Practice questions and references

References

1. www.hse.gov.uk/comah/sragtech/techmeasoperatio.htm

2. Source: The Offshore Installations (Safety Case) Regulations 2005, UK S.I. 2005/3117, 2005

3. Remotely Operated Shut-off valves, HSG244 (www.hse.gov. uk/pUbns/priced/hsg244.pdf)

Practice questions

Q1. The severity of injury received as a result of contact with electricity is minimised by:

A high current and low body resistance.

B low current and high voltage.

C low current and high body resistance.

D high current and high voltage.

Q2. What is saturated steam?

A Where all the water has been converted to steam.

B Where some liquid water is still retained in the steam.

C Steam under very high pressure.

D Steam with a temperature in excess of 200°C.

Q3. Legionellae bacteria grow at temperatures between:

A −10°C and −5°C.

B 20°C and 55°C.

C 60°C and 70°C.

D 70°C and 100°C.

Q4. One control adopted for safe start-up of plant is:

A closing of all valves.

B closing of drain valves.

C opening of all valves.

D opening of drain valves.

Q5. In terms of safety critical performance standards, what does the abbreviation 'FARSI' stand for?

A Functionality, availability, resource, survivability, interdependency.

B Functionality, asset integrity, reliability, survivability, interdependency.

C Functionality, asset integrity, reliability, systemic, interdependency.

D Functionality, availability, reliability, survivability, interdependency.

Notes

_____

_____

_____

_____

_____

_____

_____

_____

_____

_____

_____

_____

_____

_____

_____

_____

_____

_____

_____

_____

_____

_____

_____

_____

_____

_____

_____

Element 3 answers: Q1 - C; Q2 - B; Q3 - B; Q4 - B; Q5 - D.

Fire and explosion protection

Buncefield incident (picture taken by Hertfordshire Police).
©*Crown Copyright, Health and Safety Executive*

This element looks at fire and explosion hazards and how the effects can be minimised. It will also explore dust explosions and how to prevent them and will then look at reasons for developing an emergency plan.

Learning outcomes

On completion of this element, you should be able to:

4.1 Explain fire and explosion hazards relating to process industries.

4.2 Outline appropriate control measures to minimise the effects of fire and explosion in the process industries.

4.3 Outline how dusts have the potential to explode and commonly used control measures adopted to prevent and minimise explosion.

4.4 Outline the purpose and features of an emergency plan and the requirements for the implementation.

Fire hazards

1. Fire triangle and modes of heat transfer

In the process industries, fire presents a significant hazard in terms of both loss of life and property damage because of the flammable nature of many of the substances used. In order for a fire to start, there must be three elements present: **heat** (or a source of ignition), **fuel** and **oxygen**. This relationship is usually known as the 'fire triangle'.

The triangle of combustion

Fuels can be any combustible or flammable material (liquid, solid or gas) and include card, paper, petrol, oils and plastics. Heat is a source of ignition and it can come from the introduction of a spark, glowing ember from a cigarette, or from any other similar source. Oxygen is usually present in most workplaces (in the air we breathe), but may also be readily available either as compressed or liquefied oxygen (in cylinders) or in some reactive chemical compounds (called 'oxidising agents').

> **KEY TERM**
>
> **Flammable**
>
> A material that will readily catch fire if ignited by a heat source. The terms 'combustible' and 'inflammable' mean the same thing.

Simply put, if we avoid forming the fire triangle then a fire will not start in the first place, and we can use this knowledge to extinguish a fire by removing one of the sides, should a fire start. Even the most experienced fire-fighters acknowledge that the fire triangle is key in all they do.

> **ACTIVITY**
>
> In your workplace, what fuels are present? What ignition sources are present? Can these be eliminated?

If you have enough oxygen to sustain combustion, enough heat to raise the material to its ignition temperature, and fuel or combustible material, then you have the right conditions for a chemical reaction to happen. After that, fuel will ignite and, as a result, heat, light and gases will be given off in the form of fire and smoke. Some of the gases are themselves flammable and will sustain combustion.

Conduction, convection and radiation

In addition to direct burning of the material, once a fire has started, heat can be transferred by three methods: conduction, convection and radiation:

- **conduction** - the transfer of heat through solid materials. This requires direct contact between the heat and the solid material. If a pipe or girder is heated at one end, this will gradually transfer along the material until the other end is hot. By this method, heat can be transferred through buildings or other structures along structural steelwork;

- **convection** - hot fluids (liquids or gases) rise and cold fluids sink, and as this happens, heat is spread upwards from the seat of the fire. Inside buildings, this results in a hot layer of gases trapped at ceiling level, whereas outdoors, the hot gases continue to rise carrying embers away from the fire, possibly causing them to cool and fall to the ground as new ignition sources;

- **radiation** - the transfer of radiant energy from hot objects. Infrared is a type of invisible electromagnetic wave energy that radiates from hot objects. It can travel great distances and cause surfaces to heat up. These surfaces may become so hot, they burst into flames. Infrared radiation is given off by any red hot glowing material, including the sun (around half the output from the sun is infrared radiation).

In a fire, these may all be occurring at once.

2. Typical ignition sources

There are many ignition sources that could be found within the process industry, including:

- smoking;

- sparking caused from processes such as grinding, or caused by electrical short circuiting or by electrostatic discharge;

- processes involving the use of naked flames (such as oxy-acetylene welding, and also flare stacks);

- processes involving electrical discharges, eg arc welding;

- hot surfaces ranging from light bulbs to space heating and process equipment;

- mechanical friction as can be found with moving parts of equipment;

- lightning.

While it may not be possible to eliminate all of these ignition sources, the need for control of them is clear.

3. Upper flammable limit, lower flammable limit, and the risk from working within these limits

For a fire or explosion to occur, the fuel (the flammable gas or vapour) and air (the source of oxygen) need to be mixed in the right proportions or concentrations. In fact, there is a range of concentrations where ignition is possible. If the concentration of fuel is too high and there is too little oxygen, then the mixture is too fuel 'rich' and can not ignite.

Conversely, if there is too little fuel (ie the vapour concentration is too low) and too much oxygen, then the mixture is too 'lean' and can not ignite.

The highest concentration of a flammable gas or vapour in air that will ignite (when an ignition source is applied) is known as the upper flammable limit (UFL), also called the upper explosive limit (UEL). The lowest concentration of gas or vapour in air that will ignite when an ignition source is applied is known as the lower flammable limit (LFL), also called the lower explosive limit (LEL). The UEL and LEL values are usually expressed as a percentage by volume of the vapour in air. Ignition or explosion can only occur in the range between the UEL and LEL. This is known as the flammable, or explosive, range. The UEL, LEL and explosive ranges vary for each chemical according to their properties.

Explosion of acetylene in a Transit van.
HSE Science Directorate, Buxton.
©*Crown Copyright, Health and Safety Executive*

Fire hazards

| LOWER EXPLOSIVE LIMIT Insufficient fuel for combustion to occur | EXPLOSIVE RANGE | UPPER EXPLOSIVE LIMIT Insufficient air for combustion to occur |

0% Fuel, 100% Air ← Fuel (gas or vapour) to Air ratio → 100% Fuel, 0% Air

An illustration of flammable limits

Examples of flammable limits in air

Fuel	Physical State	Lower % Limit	Upper % Limit
Hydrogen	GAS	4	74
Carbon monoxide		12.5	74
Methane		5	15
Propane		2.5	9.5
Butane		2	8.5
Ethylene (ethene)		3	32
Acetylene (ethyne)		2.5	80
Ethyl alcohol (ethanol)	VAPOUR FROM LIQUID	4	19
Carbon disulphide		1.3	50
Petrol		1.4	7.5
Paraffin		0.7	5.0
Diethyl ether (ethoxyethane)		2	36

These upper and lower limits provide a guide to the control of safety. The values are determined from tests and calculations and vary with temperature, pressure and oxygen content of the air. That means you need to be careful when interpreting them and exercise a margin of safety when applying them. It is normal practice to keep concentrations of flammable gases/vapours to below 25% of their LEL/LFL to provide that margin of safety.

Clearly, if the material in question, gas/vapour or volatiles above a liquid are kept or temporarily processed at concentrations between these flammable limits, then there is a very real risk of explosion if an ignition source is present. So, it is essential to understand the risks when working within the flammable or explosive range. For example, if a petrol tank is in use, it may be that the vessel under normal conditions contains an atmospheric concentration above the UEL and so will not ignite, as it is outside the flammable range.

However, when a new tank is brought into use and filled for the first time, the introduction of petrol will initially start with an atmospheric concentration below the LEL and, as the petrol is introduced, the vessel will contain a vapour concentration within the flammable range, even if only for a short period of time. During this time, the simple action of splashing the liquid could be enough to generate a static charge and ignite the vapour.

For this reason, additional controls are usually designed in, rather than relying on the fact that the high-risk period is only brief. For abnormal events, such as leaks or releases, it is important to remember that there may be a flammable air mixture for some considerable distance from the spill until it has been diluted to below its LEL, and so exclusion zones may need to be established.

4. Mechanisms for, and possible consequences of, jet fires, pool fires, BLEVEs, CVCEs and UVCEs

When a volatile liquid ignites, the fire may progress in a number of different ways, and sometimes in more ways than one at the same time.

Jet fires

Jet fires occur when a spray of fuel is released rapidly as a stream under pressure from a process and ignited immediately on release. This results in a jet of flame being released with some considerable momentum from one or more points in the process. Jet fires can be as a result of a gas release, liquid spray (eg from fractured pipelines) or as a vapour is being forced out as it is generated.

Jets result in a high-temperature burning material being sprayed on to the installation and, as a result, can cause considerable damage very quickly. The jet may extend for a considerable distance and impact on surrounding structures and vessels, often with a great deal of momentum, and induce additional fires or cause structural collapse.

The nature of the fire depends on the pressure under which the liquid or gas is escaping, the nature of the hole size and shape, and the nature for the substance burning. Low-energy jet fires may be affected by wind, so the direction of the fire will move. Such fires tend to have a high-radiation component and their main effect will be as a result of radiated heat. High-energy discharges will act like a blowtorch and may also be very noisy with a high direct heating effect. If the jet fire is extinguished before the flow of fuel is stopped, there may be an explosion as rapidly released vapour is still venting on to hot surfaces.

Pool fires

Pool fires result from the spillage of fuel (liquids/condensate) under low pressure, which are ignited after release and the pool has developed. They may also be the result of a tank or pipe failure that has not ignited as a jet fire but has travelled out of the container to form a pool, before being ignited. It is not the liquid itself that is the pool, but the layer of vapour above the liquid and hence, when ignited, forms a pool fire. If a pool fire is not restricted to a single location, eg by being held in a bund, the liquid released may travel to another location, igniting on the way. Such fires are called 'running pool fires'. In other words, the pool is not fixed in location but moving. There is no real momentum (unlike a jet fire) and the pool fire can occur whether the spillage is on a solid surface or floating on water. A pool fire may also be involved with the ignition of vapour at the top of a storage tank, a so-called 'rim fire', which results from failure of the rim seal, or spill-over of the tank contents into the roof as a result of overpressure. When a pool fire is burning, not all the vapour may be consumed and some may blow away and form a vapour cloud that may ignite and explode.

Jet fire test, HSE Science Directorate, Buxton.
©*Crown Copyright, Health and Safety Executive*

Fire hazards

Boiling liquid expanding vapour cloud explosion (BLEVE)

Many gases, such as liquefied petroleum gas (LPG), are stored at high pressure in tanks. This enables the gas to be compressed so it forms a liquid and so takes up far less space than it would do if stored as a gas. This is extremely useful, but can also be very hazardous, if the storage vessel fails in some way. If a tank containing such a liquid is heated up, eg by involvement in a fire, the heat transfers to the contents (despite the insulation designed to protect the tank) and the contents boil, ie turn to gas. Eventually, as the liquid vaporises, the pressure in the tank increases to such a point that the pressure relief valve will operate and release the pressure to atmosphere (usually as tanks are stored in open air), the valve then closes but the heating continues.

At some point, the development of pressure in the tank will be greater than the pressure release can cope with, and where the flame of the fire is impinging directly on the metal of the tank, the heating of the tank weakens its structural integrity until the increasing pressure in the tank, from vapour expansion, causes the tank to rupture. At that point, the pressure is released instantly and there is a very high volume of rapidly expanding vapour and high-energy explosion results. This phenomenon is called a boiling liquid expanding vapour explosion, or a 'BLEVE'. It is essentially a mechanical event. The energy of the explosion can send missiles over very long distances causing significant damage. Where the contents of the tank are flammable, the vapour cloud released immediately ignites (ie as a result of the surrounding fire) and there is a secondary explosion. It can happen with any liquid under pressure, including water, and does not necessarily need a flame to weaken the tank (eg there could be a construction fault), but in the process industries, the storage of flammable and highly flammable liquids under pressure makes this of particular importance, as the secondary explosion and fire after the initial BLEVE adds to the consequences.

ACTIVITY

Watch a video of a BLEVE - there are several available, but you can find one example at:

www.youtube.com/watch?v=K-tUQTw_Vtk

Confined vapour cloud explosion (CVCE)

When a release of volatile flammable hydrocarbons occurs, it is possible, if there is sufficient quantity and the environmental conditions are right, that the vapour will form as a cloud. When the cloud reaches an ignition source, the vapour air mixture may ignite. There will be either a flash fire or an explosion, a vapour cloud explosion (VCE) - depending how quickly the flame propagates through the cloud. When this occurs in a confined area, the explosion is called a confined vapour cloud explosion (CVCE). This may be inside a building, in a reactor vessel, or a substantially enclosed space outdoors, such as created by plant structures. The excessive build-up of pressure in the confined area results in a high overpressure, shock waves and heat load. The blast wave can destroy the building itself, and the fragments of exploded vessels and other objects hit by blast waves become airborne missiles.

Unconfined vapour cloud explosion (UVCE)

When the vapour cloud forms in an unconfined space, generally outdoors, the formation and spread of the cloud depends on atmospheric conditions, such as wind speed. Such clouds may form from large loss of contents of a vessel, storage tank or pipeline. If the cloud comes into contact with a source of ignition, it may flash (ignite) or even explode. The loss of containment at Buncefield is an example of such an explosion. Thermal radiation (heat) and shock waves will be released, which can be massively destructive. This may also produce a large overpressure causing damage to the surroundings and releasing missiles as with a CVCE. Once the cloud has dispersed and is diluted below the LEL, then there is no longer a risk of ignition.

ACTIVITY

Watch the video of the Buncefield explosion developing from the evidence released during the trial - this can be found on the HSE website, at:

www.hse.gov.uk/news/buncefield/video-evidence.htm

Fire and explosion control

1. Leak and fire detection systems

Leak detection systems identify when a leak from a vessel or process line has occurred and raises the alarm. When this is used for a flammable material, this will also allow a response to be implemented (manually or automatically) in order to prevent an ignition.

Leak detectors usually comprise of a sensor system (depending on the chemical that could be potentially released) and an alarm, which will monitor the concentration of chemical in the air continuously, for example, and alarm on finding a leak. This can then allow investigation or initiate a shut-down, depending on the levels detected. There are a number of leak detection systems, many of which monitor airborne concentrations, but some can detect oil spills on to water or oil mists.

Smoke detectors detect smoke and combustion products by the disruption of a beam of light or a radiation source. The main issue with smoke detectors is their accidental operation, especially in areas where there may be dust, vapours or smokes present under normal conditions, eg in a kitchen or workshop area.

Heat detectors identify a significant increase in heat levels usually resulting from a fire, either when the heat has exceeded a set point or when there has been a rapid rate of rise in temperature that would not usually occur in the process. They usually operate when a fusible link melts, or the expansion of a material is detected.

Spot detectors are localised detectors installed at a specific point, eg in a kitchen. This means that only isolated areas may be covered by heat detectors. Line heat detectors operate differently in that a long cable is installed that can detect heat along its length and, as a result, larger areas of a process can be covered by heat detection.

Flame detectors identify the flickering or radiation emitted as a result of a fire, and trigger an alarm. The detectors can be selected to identify visible light, ultraviolet or infrared radiation given off by the fire, but these must not be blocked by structures or storage, and any processes resulting in a flash (such as welding, photography, etc) could accidentally trigger the detectors.

2. Passive fire protection, including passive protection of structures and equipment

KEY TERMS

Active fire protection

"Equipment, systems and methods, which, following initiation, may be used to control, mitigate and extinguish fires."

Passive fire protection

"coating or cladding arrangement..., which, in the event of fire, will provide thermal protection to restrict the rate at which heat is transmitted to the object or area being protected".

(Source: BS EN ISO 13702:1999[1])

Passive fire protection (PFP) systems do not require the action or intervention of a person in order to operate. It is commonly used to describe the application of coatings and the use of barriers to reduce the damage that can be caused by fire by maintaining structural integrity, or by dividing the building into fire-resistant compartments to prevent the spread of fire or smoke. The level of protection depends on the item or structure being protected.

PFP is used to maintain:

- the **integrity** of the fire compartment by preventing the spread of fire and smoke;

- the **stability** of the structure by protecting structural members, such as steelwork and girders;

- **insulation** by reducing the amount of heat transmitted during a fire.

PFP will only usually work for a limited period of time; for example, fire doors may offer 30 minutes of fire protection.

Fire and explosion control

There are many examples of PFP, some of which are found below:

- preformed boards, cladding, wall linings, etc.These are usually made from fire-resistant materials (glass, mineral or ceramic fibres) bound into cement or another fire-resistant substance;

- prefabricated walls, partitions, fire doors - structures made in a factory to be assembled on site;

- spray coatings - intumescent coatings or plasters are sprayed on to structural steelwork, etc to act as a barrier to reduce the risk of damage by heat and fire;

- seals and sealants - intumescent seals are used to prevent the spread of smoke and fire, both around doors and used around pipes and cables that have penetrated a fire compartment (wall).

KEY TERM

Intumescent

A material that expands when heated and, as a result, fills a space and prevents the spread of fire and smoke. One common place to find an intumescent seal is around a fire door.

3. Active fire protection systems

Active fire protection (AFP) is any system that detects fire and activates in order to mitigate or extinguish fire. These can be fixed installations (such as sprinklers) or portable (such as extinguishers), automatic (triggered by a detector) or manual (operated by a person, such as on the activation of a call point).

Some examples of AFP can be found below:

- sprinkler systems - a water-based sprinkler system requires a readily available source of water, often from a storage tank, to assure a supply of water, a fire pump designed to provide the water at the designed flow rate, and fire water mains to carry the water to the sprinkler heads. Sprinkler heads can be operated by the detectors or by the melting of a glass bulb;

- foam sprinklers - sprinkler systems can also be charged with water-based foam rather than just water. This requires the use of a foam additive into the system, but can be highly effective against hydrocarbon or other flammable liquid fires;

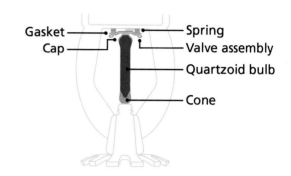

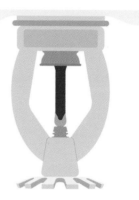

Schematic of a fixed installation water sprinkler

- gas-extinguishing systems - in these systems, fire detection triggers the release of an inert gas such as carbon dioxide (as used in portable extinguishers) to smother and extinguish the fire. This can be used safely on fires involving electrical equipment.

KEY TERM

Inert

Chemically inactive. An inert gas will not react or sustain a fire and so can be used to eliminate oxygen and so prevent the formation of an explosive atmosphere. The most common inert gas used is nitrogen.

THOUGHT PROVOKER

While sprinklers are highly effective, the damage that can result from accidental operation is not to be underestimated and, therefore, controls need to be in place to avoid accidental damage. Think about ways in which the sprinkler head can be damaged or accidentally operated in a warehouse or factory.

All active fire protection systems do, however, require regular testing and maintenance to ensure that they remain reliable.

4. Zoning/hazardous area classification and selection of suitable equipment

If there is an atmosphere that could be flammable due to the presence of explosive dusts or vapours, then the electrical and mechanical equipment used in the area must be carefully selected to prevent ignition. In Europe, there are two directives that cover this:

- ATEX 95 Equipment Directive covers the supply of equipment for use in flammable atmospheres;

- ATEX 137 Workplace Directive covers the safety of workers in these areas.

In electrical area classification, areas where flammable dusts or vapours are handled are classified into zones based on the potential for a flammable atmosphere to be present.

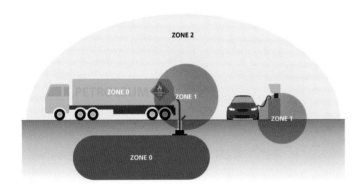

Adapted from: www.enggcyclopedia.com/2011/10/
hazardous-area-classification[2]

Area classification - zone definitions for explosive dusts

Under the EU Directive 99/92/EC (also known as ATEX 137 or the ATEX Workplace Directive), there is a requirement to classify areas where there could be dusts or vapours present in explosive concentrations. This standard is therefore commonly adopted:

- for flammable vapours:

  - zone 0 - a place in which an explosive atmosphere is present continuously, or for long periods or frequently;

  - zone 1 - a place in which an explosive atmosphere is likely to occur in normal operation occasionally;

  - zone 2 - a place in which an explosive atmosphere is not likely to occur in normal operation, but if it does occur, will persist for a short period only.

- For flammable dusts:

  - zone 20 - a place in which an explosive atmosphere in the form of a cloud of combustible dust in air is present continuously, or for long periods or frequently;

  - zone 21 - a place in which an explosive atmosphere in the form of a cloud of combustible dust in air is likely to occur in normal operation occasionally;

  - zone 22 - a place in which an explosive atmosphere in the form of a cloud of combustible dust in air is not likely to occur in normal operation, but if it does occur, will persist for a short period only.

Different standards of electrical equipment will be needed in different zones:

Electrical Equipment	Zone
Category 1	Zone 0 or Zone 20
Category 2	Zone 1 or Zone 21
Category 3	Zone 2 or Zone 22

Category 1 equipment can be used in all zones, Category 2 equipment can be used in Zones 1 or 2, and Category 3 equipment can only be used in Zone 2.

Equipment for use in a flammable atmosphere is commonly known as 'intrinsically safe' and will be marked with this symbol:

There are many different types of intrinsically safe equipment, from sealed to resin-filled and even gas inerted, but the detail is not necessary for this course.

It is not only electrical equipment that must be selected to be safe for use in flammable atmospheres; some mechanical equipment could generate sufficient heat or sparks (especially under faulty conditions) to ignite a flammable atmosphere. Control equipment (such as computers and monitors) that may be exposed to a flammable atmosphere may need to be protected by an alternative means, such as the use of a sealed nitrogen-inerted cabinet in the event that a suitable, intrinsically safe item of equipment can not be sourced.

Fire and explosion control

5. Explosion protection systems

Clearly, it is the intention that fire and explosion are prevented, but if a risk remains, then suitable protection systems must be in place to protect lives and plant:

- atmosphere control - here, the atmosphere is managed through the introduction of an inert gas, such as nitrogen or carbon dioxide, in order to exclude oxygen and prevent the formation of a flammable mixture;

- pressure relief/explosion venting - a point of weakness is built into the process or vessel. It is designed to relieve at a pressure that is far below the pressure that would cause damage to the vessel, and this results in the release of any pressure build-up in a safe manner to a safe location. The relief must be to a safe location and not into an occupied area and, as such, explosion vents are carefully designed. Pressure relief can be via hinged doors that swing open, explosion panels, or commonly in the form of a 'bursting disc', which is a single-use disc of metal carefully designed to rupture at a set pressure (and can be replaced if activated);

- automatic explosion suppression - this involves the use of a detector and an inert media, such as dry powder. When a build-up of pressure is detected, the rapid introduction of a suppressant can prevent the development of the explosion;

- automatic isolation - here, when a fire is detected, the system automatically cuts off the flammable liquid, feeding the area in order to prevent development of the fire. At Piper Alpha, there was no such process in operation and, as a result, the fuel continued to be pumped to the rig, exacerbating the incident and increasing the scale of the disaster;

- flame arrestors - a flame arrestor allows gas to pass through it, but is designed to stop a flame in order to prevent an explosion. The first example of a flame arrestor was the Davy Lamp, a safety lamp developed for miners in 1815. The basic principle is that the lamp (and flame arrestors that followed) utilise a mesh screen with holes too fine to allow the flame to propagate through it. The progress of the flame through the fine mesh cools the gas/air mixture and stops combustion.

Buncefield Oil Refinery, fire and explosion incident.
©*Crown Copyright, Health and Safety Executive*

Modern flame arrestors can be installed either in-line along pipelines (preventing flames from passing through the pipeline to the rest of the process) or as end-of-line devices on lines that vent to atmosphere; in the event that the venting vapour is ignited, the flame is prevented from spreading back into the vessel.

Flame arrestors are a passive isolation system; in the event that a fire is detected, there will be active systems in place to prevent fires, such as the monitoring of the oxygen level and the introduction of an inert blanket as we have already seen, but in the event that these fail, the passive flame arrestor will operate to protect the plant and process.

6. Benefits and limitations of chemical, foam and inert extinguishing systems

As we have already touched upon, there is a variety of extinguishing media available for fire-fighting, either in small portable extinguishers or in large, fixed installations. There are benefits and limitations to each:

- dry chemical extinguishing systems - here, a dry powder is used, propelled by a pressurised gas canister to smother the fire. This can be highly effective against hydrocarbon fires, including jet fires and running pool fires, but as the liquid remains heated there is a potential for re-ignition. They are also extremely messy and can result in significant damage, eg if the powder enters electrical equipment, it will usually be inoperable;

- foam systems - here, a foam concentrate is added to water in a system to produce a chemical foam that is used to smother a fire. This can be used on a hydrocarbon pool fire but will not be effective on a jet fire. As the fire is smothered by a blanket of foam, the fire will be extinguished, unless the blanket is incomplete and the surface of the liquid is again exposed to the air - there can then be a re-ignition, although the foam does also provide a cooling effect;

- inert gas - here, an inert gas such as carbon dioxide is discharged into a room or vessel if a fire is detected, smothering the fire and removing the oxygen. The real advantage of this system over dry powder extinguishers or foam is that the equipment in the area will be largely unaffected (except that which was involved in the fire obviously!). The greatest concern is the risk of asphyxiation if someone is trapped in the room when the system activates, so there must be stringent controls, eg an audible alarm and an override.

7. Examples of fire protection systems for tank farms

Tank farms can be protected using water- or foam-based deluge systems that act to extinguish fires. A deluge system is similar to a sprinkler system, but the water flow is higher and from all heads in the system, not just a selected few.

Water monitors (very high flow water or foam jets) can also be installed as a fixed or portable system to fight fires. These systems can also be used in the event of a fire near to the tank farm, to provide a cooling curtain or water to prevent heat being transferred by radiation on to the tanks.

8. Mitigation of lightning strikes

Lightning is another ignition source that needs to be managed within the process industry. In order to protect plant from lightning strikes, there should be a lightning rod attached to the highest point of the plant that is attached to a continuous metal cable or wire and then into an earth rod, a metal stake driven into the earth. The electrical continuity of the lightning rod should be tested to ensure that it provides an unbroken path to earth, so that if lightning does strike, it is dissipated safely without passing through the structure of the building. Within the plant, other electrical structures and equipment should be connected to the earth connection to dissipate any static generated, eg by the flow of solvents within pipework.

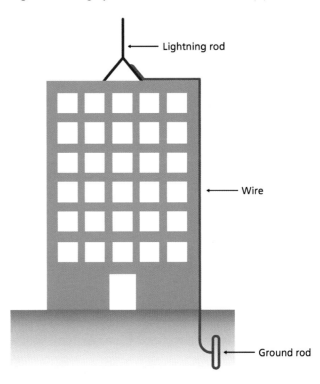

Diagram of a simple lightning protection system

Dust explosions

1. Why dust explosions occur

Dust explosions happen when a combustible dust with the correct particle size forms a cloud of the right concentration in air. This dust is known as 'explosible'. Combustible dusts include some commonly found materials, such as flour, sugar, milk powder, coal and grain. Dust explosions can occur in processes where there are dusts handled, such as grain silos, extraction systems, spray driers and material transfer systems.

The following conditions are needed for dusts to become explosible:

- particle size - a combustible dust must have a fine enough particle size to sufficiently increase the surface area;

- dispersal - the dust must be in a combustible mixture in the air (similar to the explosive mixture needed for flammable vapours);

- explosive concentrations - unlike flammable vapours, dusts do not have a defined LEL and UEL, but as an indicative value, the LEL would be 25-50g per cubic metre of air, with UEL ten times the LEL. At these concentrations, the dust cloud would be heavy and clearly apparent;

- ignition energy - there is a minimum ignition energy (MIE) required in order to ignite the dust. This data is usually available for each dust and is critical in the assessment of explosion risk;

- heat and humidity - high temperatures can increase the risk of dust explosion as hot surfaces can ignite the dust if they provide the MIE. High humidity (damping down), on the other hand, can reduce the likelihood of a dust explosion as dust clouds do not form as readily, and a greater MIE is needed to ignite the dust.

We have already seen that, for fires to start, the fire triangle is essential: heat, fuel and oxygen are needed. In order to create the conditions for a dust explosion, the 'dust pentagon' considers heat, fuel, oxygen, confinement of the dust (eg enclosing the dust within a building or silo) and dispersion of the dust (formation of the dust cloud).

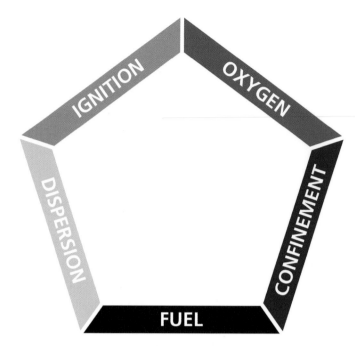

The dust pentagon

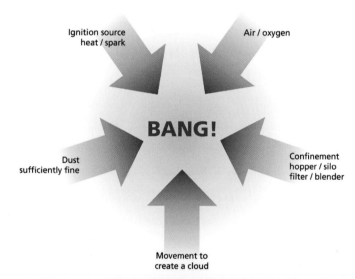

ACTIVITY

Are there any combustible dusts in use in your workplace? What about in your kitchen? If we handle combustible dusts in the home, eg while baking, why are there not dust explosions happening in homes every day?

ELEMENT 1
ELEMENT 2
ELEMENT 3
ELEMENT 4

2. Primary and secondary explosions

As we have seen, the conditions needed for dust explosions to occur are fairly prescribed. It is unusual for such conditions, eg explosive concentrations of dust, to be present in the general atmosphere as these would, at a basic level, need to be controlled for operator exposure and health issues! As a result, most dust explosions happen within processes or equipment where conditions for the explosion can be achieved more readily. These explosions are known as 'primary explosions'. The primary explosion can be quite minor in itself, but the dust disturbed within the building (eg on the floor, girders, lying on vessels, etc) then forms an explosible mixture and is ignited, causing one or more secondary explosions that can be devastating. Housekeeping and dust control is therefore essential in any area where process dusts are generated.

ACTIVITY

Watch the video "Inferno: Dust explosion at Imperial Sugar" produced by the Chemical Safety Board (CSB) at www.csb.gov. Identify the potential ignition sources and reasons for the incident.

3. Prevention of dust explosions

Risk assessment

In order to prevent a dust explosion, it is essential that the conditions needed for an explosion are understood and the potential assessed so that controls can be implemented. This will occur through the development of a robust risk assessment process.

The HSE publication HSG103 *Safe handling of combustible dusts: precautions against explosion*[3] states that, once a risk assessment has been carried out, actions should be taken using this simple hierarchy:

- eliminate the risk;

- use controls to prevent explosions;

- provide controls to mitigate the risk.

Elimination and reduction of dusts at source

The first step of the risk assessment is to identify any potentially explosive dusts. The most effective control would be to eliminate the generation of dusts, where possible, by the use of alternative techniques, such as the replacement of dusts with slurries (solids suspended in liquids), pastes or emulsions. Where the handling of dry ingredients is necessary, then handling the material in granular or pastille form will reduce the potential for dusts to be generated (although some smaller quantities may still be present).

THOUGHT PROVOKER

A chemical plant experienced a minor dust explosion while charging catalyst material to a mixer. After extensive investigation into technical controls to prevent explosible mixtures, it was decided to ask if the supplier could provide the catalyst in a wet form. Not only was this safer, it removed the need for thousands of dollars worth of control measures. Safety does not have to be complex, sometimes, the simplest solutions are the best.

Inerting

We saw earlier that one element essential for fire or explosion is oxygen. Inerting is the process of blanketing or flooding a vessel with an inert gas, such as nitrogen, to exclude oxygen and so prevent the formation of a flammable or explosive atmosphere. Inerting can only be used in enclosed processes or vessels, and as the atmosphere is irrespirable (in that it can not sustain life), stringent controls must be in place to ensure worker safety, especially during maintenance. As there may be a number of opportunities for air to enter the process, (eg on addition of raw materials, through sampling ports, etc), careful assessment and calculations must be carried out to ensure that oxygen is sufficiently excluded.

Dust extraction systems

Appropriate dust extraction systems can be used to remove and contain dusts at source and, again, minimise fugitive releases. Any dust extraction system must be specifically designed for a purpose and incorporate suitable filters or other air purification devices, in order to ensure dusts are contained and that there are no parts that could ignite a flammable atmosphere.

Dust explosions

Good housekeeping

Another example of simple solutions is to maintain an environment where there is little or no dust lying on surfaces through good housekeeping. This will reduce the risk of secondary explosions occurring. Housekeeping can be improved, firstly, by enclosing processes to contain fugitive dust emissions, and then to provide a cleaning regime that removes dust from surfaces to prevent accumulation. Damp dusting and vacuuming (with appropriately rated electrical equipment to prevent ignition!) should be carried out in preference to sweeping, which in itself generates dust clouds.

Avoidance of ignition sources

Equipment for use in areas that could contain a potentially explosive concentration requires careful selection of electrical and mechanical equipment, to ensure that there are no ignition sources present. This could be from electrical sparks, hot surfaces, static, etc. These areas are commonly referred to as 'zoned areas'.

It is common in any zoned area to control hot work and other works that could generate a spark but, in addition, any equipment installed, electrical or non-electrical, should be appropriately rated for use in that area.

4. Mitigation of dust explosions

Mitigation measures accept that a potential for an explosion remains, so measures are put in place to minimise the impact, either by controlling the explosion and resulting pressure wave, or by suppressing the explosion and preventing a secondary explosion.

Explosion relief venting

Explosion relief venting is the inclusion of points of weakness within the process or equipment so that, in the event that there is an explosion, the resultant pressure is vented to a safe location. This is the most common mitigation measure found for dust explosions. As a dust explosion can result in a jet flame, the vent must relieve the pressure into a safe location, eg through a duct and not into an occupied building. The size and type of relief panel needed is determined through calculations, and this should be carried out by a competent engineer.

Explosion suppression and containment

Explosion containment simply refers to building plant that is sufficiently strong to contain the pressure generated during a dust explosion. As these pressures can be significant, most plant and equipment are unlikely to safely contain an explosion. Explosion suppression systems, on the other hand, use a pressure detector to rapidly identify the start of an explosion and inject a suppressant material into the plant to stop the explosion developing. The suppressant is usually dry powder similar to that found in portable fire extinguishers.

Plant siting and construction

Where there is still a risk of dust explosion, then the location of plant and equipment in the open air may be desirable. If this is not possible, then any pressure must vent to a safe location, ideally externally to the building and in any circumstances not into an occupied area.

If the building is constructed of brick or stone (or other robust materials), in the event of a secondary explosion within the building, the walls may collapse, causing serious injuries or fatalities. It is therefore usual to construct buildings of light-weight materials or containing panels that can easily (and intentionally) collapse (or 'blow out') to relieve pressure without resulting in a collapse.

Where plant is connected (eg storage silos, weight hoppers, charge hoppers, mixers, bagging plant, etc), there may need to be suppression or venting systems designed into the process to prevent a dust explosion travelling from one part of the process to the next, and to reduce the risk.

UN series explosives "sandbox" detonation test, HSE Science Directorate, Buxton.
©*Crown Copyright, Health and Safety Executive*

Emergency preparedness

1. Purpose of an emergency plan

It is a fact that, despite the best controls, sometimes emergencies do happen, and that is when the organisations and individuals reap the benefits of thorough emergency planning. Emergency planning can cover a range of response levels, from simple first aid to full off-site evacuations for the most serious incidents. The level that is required is often determined by the legal requirements.

An emergency plan should be developed so that, in the event that there is an emergency, the actions and controls that follow are established and planned, understood by all involved and that the roles and responsibilities are clear. This will ensure that care is given rapidly to any injured parties and that all on-site and off-site impacts are mitigated.

2. Development of an emergency plan

Some legislation, for example the Control of Major Accident Hazards Regulations 2015 (COMAH), requires the development of safety cases and the preparation of a Major Accident Prevention Policy (MAPP), explored earlier in Element 2. In any case, an emergency plan is a formal, written document that identifies the potential hazards, the steps to be taken to control any emergency events and the roles and responsibilities for delivering the response.

A significant part of the development of any emergency plan is the identification of possible emergency scenarios.

Identification of possible scenarios and response

The type of emergencies that should be considered in the emergency plan depends very much on the hazard profile of the organisation and the types of foreseeable event that could occur. Examples may include:

- first aid;

- medical incident (an event requiring more than first aid, for installations without ready access to the emergency services);

- fire or explosion;

- loss of containment (chemical spillage, toxic gas release);

- bomb threat or terrorism;

- outbreak of disease or illness (eg norovirus within a closed community, such as on an oil rig);

- flooding or adverse weather event.

Not all organisations will need to consider all of the above incidents, and some additional ones, eg radiological release, may be pertinent to specialist industries. So, it is important that the plan is developed for the site by those with knowledge of the processes, based on the probability that each emergency event will occur and the potential consequences if it does. Focusing on realistic scenarios rather than doomsday predictions that are highly unlikely to arise; for example, a site located on a river or flood plain should realistically consider flooding as a potential event, whereas for other locations, any flooding is only likely to occur locally if storm drains are overwhelmed.

Selection of those involved in plan development

Any on-site response should be developed utilising the available local knowledge and expertise of workers at all levels. Experienced plant operators and managers alike may have a role to play, but engineers and specialists, such as health and safety or environmental professionals, may also be able to assist in the development of the plan.

The level of off-site and external involvement will largely be dictated by legislation, but it is beneficial to engage with external parties who may be involved in a real incident wherever possible. Examples include:

- regulators;

- local authorities and councils;

- water companies and authorities;

- utility companies;

- emergency services, including the police and fire service.

These parties may not only have valuable insight that can be shared during the development of the plan, but also may be involved in the event that the plan is put into action during an incident, and so would benefit from being familiar with the site, its hazards and procedures.

Emergency preparedness

Senior managers can also play an important role in the emergency plan as there may be a need to manage contact with families (next of kin) for injured parties, and manage media and regulator communications.

Resources based on likelihood and consequence of events

The level of resource needed will differ, depending on the events that could occur and the likelihood and consequence of each. For example, most onshore organisations would have a first-aid provision, with basic facilities, first-aid trained workers and perhaps a first-aid room. Additional controls may be added, such as automated external defibrillators (AEDs), oxygen therapy and use of evacuation chairs if that is felt to be relevant, but this is still within the usual remit of a first-aid team (albeit with additional training).

Some sites may benefit from establishing a centralised emergency control room. This could be stocked with all of the equipment needed during an incident. This could include computer, printer, radios, phones, plans and maps, material safety data sheets, contact numbers, etc.

External emergency response and their availability

When developing the emergency plan, it is important to identify if the emergency service response is likely to be delayed due to location of the site (eg offshore wind farms, isolated chemical plants or oil rigs). In these circumstances, the level of expertise needed may be increased and includes the provision of advanced trauma care, on-site emergency response teams capable of rescuing a casualty using breathing apparatus, confined space rescue teams, rescue at heights trained workers, etc.

It is also possible that, due to the specialist nature of the chemicals and processes handled, the site needs to provide trained workers able to assist with the emergency services response on arrival to the site. At a very basic level, any first responders will require information on any chemicals or other hazards present so that they can ensure the safety of their own crews deployed into the incident. Specialist chemical teams, for example, may not be available locally and may be some time in responding.

On-site medical facilities and the availability of off-site facilities

Most facilities will offer basic first-aid treatment and trained first-aid workers but, in specialist industries, or ones in isolated locations as we have started to explore already, additional controls may be needed.

It is not usual to provide a high level of medical facility unless there are no such provisions in the local area - in the developed world, this is rarely the case and emergency care can usually be obtained, although there may be a delay while waiting for helicopter transport from an oil rig, for instance. On-site teams are now commonly trained in the use of AEDs to support first-aid resuscitation training, but they may be provided with additional training to enable them to deliver trauma care if the risk assessment deems it necessary. In addition, if there are hazardous chemicals, such as hydrofluoric acid, then the delivery of antidotes may be necessary, but again this should only be carried out with specialist training.

Requirement for on-site and off-site emergency plans

KEY TERMS

On-site plan

An internal plan detailing the site's emergency response; it may include the need to contact the emergency services or regulators externally but this is an internal plan as it is delivered by site workers.

Off-site plan

The off-site response to an incident which will be developed by external agencies, in order to provide a co-ordinated response to an incident.

The need for off-site plans will usually be identified in applicable legislation, and usually only high-hazard installations will require an off-site plan. Where there is a requirement for both plans to be developed, they should fit together and ensure the smooth running of an incident and any subsequent off-site response, such as road closures and residential evacuations. Both plans should contain actions for the immediate response to the incident and longer-term recovery and response actions.

ELEMENT 1

ELEMENT 2

ELEMENT 3

ELEMENT 4

We can use the COMAH regulations as an example here as they contain information as to the contents of the emergency plans.

Part 1 of Schedule 4 states that an on-site plan should contain the following:

(a) the name or position of -
   (i) any person authorised to set emergency procedures in motion; and
   (ii) the person in charge of and co-ordinating the mitigatory action within the establishment;

(b) the name or position of the person with responsibility for liaising with the local authority responsible for the external emergency plan;

(c) for foreseeable conditions or events which could be significant in bringing about a major accident, a description of the action which should be taken to control the conditions or events and to limit their consequences, including a description of the safety equipment and the resources available;

(d) the arrangements for limiting the risks to persons within the establishment including how warnings are to be given and the actions persons are expected to take on receipt of a warning;

(e) the arrangements for providing early warning of an incident to the local authority responsible for setting the external emergency plan in motion, the type of information which should be contained in an initial warning and the arrangements for the provision of more detailed information as it becomes available;

(f) where necessary, the arrangements for training staff in the duties they will be expected to perform and, as appropriate, co-ordinating this with the emergency services;

(g) the arrangements for providing assistance with mitigatory action outside the establishment.

Part 1 of Schedule 4 states that an off-site plan should contain the following:

(a) the name or position of -
   (i) any person authorised to set emergency procedures in motion; and
   (ii) any person authorised to take charge of and co-ordinate action outside the establishment;

(b) the arrangements for receiving early warning of incidents, and alert and call-out procedures;

(c) the arrangements for co-ordinating resources necessary to implement the external emergency plan; (d) the arrangements

(d) the arrangements for providing assistance with mitigatory action within the establishment;

(e) the arrangements for mitigatory action outside the establishment, including responses to major accident scenarios as set out in the safety report and considering possible domino effects, including those having an impact on the environment;

(f) the arrangements for providing the public and any neighbouring establishments or sites that fall outside the scope of these Regulations in accordance with regulation 24 (domino effects and domino groups) with specific information relating to an accident and the behaviour which should be adopted;

(g) the arrangements for the provision of information to the emergency services of other Member States in the event of a major accident with possible trans-boundary consequences.

(Source: L111 (Third edition): *The Control Of Major Accident Hazards Regulations 2015, Guidance on Regulations* [4])

Emergency preparedness

3. Content of an emergency plan

As we have already explored, the content of an emergency plan will differ depending on the hazard potential of the site, so now we will consider some general requirements and how they may apply to different workplaces.

Systems for alerting and warning workers

Most organisations will require a means of alerting on-site workers to the presence of an incident. At the basic level this could be a fire alarm, but for some installations the alarm may need to include:

- separate alarms for fire and chemical release;

- staged evacuation of the facility, with some areas evacuating while others remain operational;

- first aid and medical emergency alerts;

- off-site alarms to alert local businesses and residents.

THOUGHT PROVOKER

At a visit to an industrial premises, part of the induction included the necessary response to a gas alarm from an adjacent facility. All businesses and residents in the area were informed of action to be taken on hearing the gas alarm and this was passed to contractors and visitors and reinforced with the use of signs and alarm tests.

Such a system was sadly not in place at Bohpal in India in 1984, when a methyl isocyanate release from the Union Carbide chemical plant occurred; the failure to alert residents in the immediate vicinity to the plant dramatically affected the death toll as there was no procedure to evacuate the local area, and officially 2259 were killed but the death toll is not known fully.

Responsibilities in the event of an emergency

Leadership is essential in the event of an emergency situation, without leadership, the incident may not be safely managed and could escalate rather than being brought to a safe conclusion.

In some circumstances, there may be a senior manager on site 24 hours a day, seven days a week, but this is not always the case. In out-of-hours times, the control must pass smoothly to a person who will always be present, such as a shift supervisor or similar. In all circumstances, however, those who could potentially act in a leadership role must be suitably trained and competent to:

- ask pertinent and challenging questions to determine the best course of action;

- make critical decisions based on information available and be able to stand back where necessary and safest to do so;

- manage the actions of the on-site emergency teams and first aiders;

- manage interactions with regulators and emergency services.

Once the incident has been identified and 'declared', it may be possible to call in additional workers to support the team managing the incident. This major incident team could involve senior managers, human resources (to contact families of those affected), health and safety professionals and directors who could be considering business continuity, etc.

Expertise of teams responding to an incident

All on-site workers who could be involved in incident response need to be suitably trained, and this will be covered later in this section. The selection of those with key roles should, however, take into consideration the potential to utilise specialist skills, such as:

- engineers who can assist with problem-solving and control of releases;

- health and safety professionals for practical and legal guidance;

- operators for practical information on the running and operation of the equipment;

- supervisors for more detailed knowledge of the plant and processes;

- chemists for specialist knowledge, eg about reactions that could occur with water, advice on safety data sheet contents, etc.

Where there are a number of processes operating on site, consideration should be given to ensuring that the person leading the incident has the best possible level of skill and experience in the process affected, or is supported by those with specialist knowledge of the plant.

Managing the expertise of the external response to the incident is not usually possible, but for high-hazard installations, the emergency services may carry out familiarisation visits to understand the layout, hazards and processes that are operated. Regulators and authorities may also be in attendance on occasion as part of the development of any off-site emergency plans.

In all incidents involving chemicals, all first responders (fire, ambulance, police, etc) will require critical information from the relevant safety data sheets and this must therefore be rapidly and readily available.

ACTIVITY

Think about potential incidents on your site:

- Who takes the lead during the incident? Are they on site 24/7 or are they called in?

- What training have they received?

- What specialists are utilised? How are they contacted?

Evacuation and shelter arrangements

Procedures need to be established to evacuate areas of the site affected by an emergency. This could be a partial evacuation or a full-site response. The Chemical Industries Association (CIA) has produced guidance[5] on the location and design of occupied buildings, which could prove useful in assisting with the development of emergency procedures.

The evacuation procedures must be tailored to the nature of the hazard, for example:

- a fire evacuation may be initially to an on-site muster point, with an off-site secondary point established in the event of a more serious incident;

- a toxic gas alarm may result in the need for workers to enter gas refuges within the building, rather than responding to an external emergency muster point. In these circumstances, mechanical ventilation, eg air-conditioning systems, may need to be shutdown to avoid drawing in contaminants;

- a full off-site evacuation procedure which results in the workers leaving site may be required under extreme conditions and a suitable assembly point, such as a local sports hall, club or hotel, may be possible.

If there is the potential for off-site workers, such as residents, to be evacuated then the emergency plan should give consideration to where these people can be moved to as a place of safety, and how sleeping facilities and food can be provided if the incident takes some time to resolve or happens overnight.

Emergency shut-down of plant and services

There needs to be the on-site knowledge and ability to isolate and shut-down:

- process plant that may be operational;

- electrical services;

- gas and chemical supplies;

- hot oil and heating systems;

- drains and sewers to contain spillages or fire water.

As a minimum, most facilities have plans and drawings within their emergency plan that detail the location of isolation valves, drains and sewers, electrical isolation points, etc. These can then be operated by internal workers if safe to do so, or by the emergency services on provision of the relevant information and while wearing appropriate PPE.

In some circumstances, it may be necessary for critical workers to remain in control rooms, in order to carry out safe shut-down of plant, eg chemical reactions need to be controlled and many can not be simply 'switched off' or they may accelerate and cause an additional emergency. If this is the case, the control room operator must be monitored and only remain in situ if it is safe to do so.

Emergency preparedness

Vulnerable people

Some groups are considered to be vulnerable during an emergency situation and, as such, may need specific consideration in the emergency plan. Personal Emergency Evacuation Plans (PEEPs) may be developed for those who need assistance in an emergency, such as those with hearing impairment who may not be aware of the alarm, those with visual impairment who may require assistance or those in wheelchairs which, in some circumstances, may need to utilise disabled refuges or evacuation chairs in the event of a fire alarm.

Systems for accounting for workers

There should be a robust process in place to account for all workers in the event of an emergency. This often takes the place of an automatic or manual roll-call system.

KEY TERM

Roll call

A process similar to reading the school register during which every person registered on site is checked to ensure that they have assembled at the muster point.

A manual roll call uses workers to manually read out the names of workers or visitors to site and to ask if they are present at the muster point. In the event that a person is identified as missing, this can be highlighted and investigated.

An automatic roll call operates using a computerised system, such as a swipe card or key fob; each worker swipes as they enter the site and on leaving and that establishes a record of those present at any time. In an emergency, there may be an additional swipe point at the assembly point which allows people to indicate that they are safe and so a summary can be produced showing those not accounted for.

Discussion between HSE inspector and nuclear operative, Sellafield.
©*Crown Copyright, Health and Safety Executive*

4. Information management and media liaison

Information management is critical during any incident, from the minute the incident is declared until the incident is concluded, information will be flowing throughout the team, so there must be processes in place to manage it. These may include:

- real-time information on the incident as it develops (details of plant, processes, materials involved, etc and decisions made). This can be recorded in a chronological log, sometimes on a whiteboard at the emergency control centre;

- hazard information essential for the emergency services, eg material safety data sheets, which must be readily available, in an understandable format and in the correct local language;

- details of casualties, including next-of-kin contacts; this can be managed by human resources or personnel managers;

- information for the regulators - external reporting may be necessary;

- media relations - media can be utilised to assist in the evacuation of an area, but more usually can respond to reports of an incident seeking statements. If the site is to establish a media response then workers at the appropriate level must be trained in media skills to avoid media distortion of events and prevent unintentional alarm being caused.

After the incident, reports will need to be made to identify root causes and lessons learnt, and these can be developed using the information collated during the event.

5. Theoretical training

One approach to emergency training is the use of theoretical, classroom-based sessions that involve the use of tabletop exercises. These are useful as they can improve engagement and sharpen decision-making skills, but unlike the practical exercises they are relatively quick and simple to set up and, as a result, a few scenarios can be carried out in a short session.

KEY TERM

Tabletop exercise

A classroom-based scenario presented as a theoretical incident that the groups respond to in their team roles. They run through the incident in an accelerated timeframe, stating the information they would need, actions they would take and react in turn to information provided by the trainer.

Any gaps or deficiencies in the response during the tabletop exercises can be addressed and further activities carried out to determine if the issues have been solved satisfactorily.

6. Competency of response team and commanders

The response team and the incident commanders must all be competent to carry out their roles. We have already discussed the importance of technical competence of the team but, in addition, there is a clear need to ensure that those placed in response roles have the additional skills that they require to deal with an incident:

- incident commanders - they need the experience of leading and managing a team and the authority to do so under considerable pressure. It is also essential that they are able to stand back and analyse the situation and not risk the safety of workers if waiting for the emergency services is most appropriate. Good communication skills are essential, as is the ability to recognise that the most effective leaders are not physically involved in the incident, but are standing back commanding rather than clearing up the spillage, for example;

- response team members - they will not only have site experience, but also have the training and skills to safely wear breathing apparatus, carry out basic fire-fighting or deliver first aid (depending on their training and site policies).

Emergency preparedness

THOUGHT PROVOKER

It is important to fit the right person into the right role - someone who is naturally shy might not be suited to taking the roll call for a busy industrial site.

Competence is a blend of knowledge, skills and experience; while we hope that few response team members have had lots of emergency situations to practise on, the role of simulation training can not be underestimated, and this we will consider next.

7. Practical emergency-scenario testing

While theoretical training has a part to play, there is no real substitute for practical drills and exercises, carried out in real time and using the workers who would respond in a real emergency in their response team roles. These can be carried out at a number of different levels:

- fire or emergency evacuation drill - a basic test of emergency response. The alarm is triggered and workers respond as they would in an emergency. This tests the response of workers and visitors, fire wardens, roll-call effectiveness and the audibility of alarms across the site;

- response team drill - a mock scenario is set up, eg a tanker spillage, and the alarm is sounded to the group under training only. They then respond in roles and deal with the incident in real time, with information being supplied by the trainers or organiser as the event escalates. This has the benefit of testing the actual response, rather than the theoretical response to an incident. It is easy to say, "I would wear a respirator", but when watching a practical drill it is possible to see if the worker is firstly able to obtain the respirator, select the right filter, wear it correctly, ensure their own safety, and so on, which would not be apparent from a tabletop exercise. These exercises can be challenging, but also very enjoyable as the teams develop and improve their skills and so the confidence of the group grows. In this drill, the emergency services are not actually contacted, but workers or trainers may take on those roles in order to test and practise the communication skills needed;

- full-site emergency response drill - sometimes, there is a regulatory requirement to test the on-site and off-site response by carrying out a multidisciplinary drill involving regulators, emergency services, local authorities, etc. This is a very onerous and involved undertaking that may also require the full evacuation of the site and so requires a great deal of organisation and can be costly.

ACTIVITY

When did you last hold an emergency drill on site? What did it involve? What conclusions were drawn and what action was taken as a result?

8. Provision of information to the public

The regulators may determine that members of the public in the vicinity of a hazardous installation need to be provided with information, eg the response to take in the event of an alarm and the potential hazards. In addition, during a major incident, there may also be a need to provide factual information to those potentially affected in order to avoid rumour, panic and alarm. To this end, emergency control centres should be suitably equipped to allow these communications to be carried out smoothly.

References

1. BS EN ISO 13702:1999 Petroleum and natural gas industries. Control and mitigation of fires and explosions on offshore production installations. Requirements and guidelines

2. Hazardous area classification (www.enggcyclopedia.com/2011/10/)

3. HSG103 Safe handling of combustible dusts: precautions against explosion

4. L111 (Third edition): The Control Of Major Accident Hazards Regulations 2015, Guidance on Regulations

5. www.cia.org.uk/AboutUs/OrderPublications/Publicationdetails/tabid/146/pubctl/DetailPublication/ID/12/Default.aspx

Practice questions

Q1. Which of the following best describes a Zone 1 hazardous area?

A   A place in which an explosive mixture in the form of a cloud of combustible dust in air is likely to occur in normal operation occasionally.

B   A place in which an explosive atmosphere in the form of a cloud of flammable gas in air is likely to occur in normal operation occasionally.

C   A place in which an explosive atmosphere in the form of a cloud of combustible dust in air is not likely to occur in normal operation, but if it does occur, will persist for a short period only.

D   A place in which an explosive atmosphere in the form of a flammable gas in air is not likely to occur in normal operation, but if it does occur, will persist for a short period only.

Q2. An external fire directly heats a vessel containing a flammable liquid. The liquid begins to boil, increasing the pressure which opens an integral pressure relief valve. The liquid level inside the vessel lowers and the fire now begins to heat the vessel above the liquid level. The vessel metal thins, weakens and ruptures. What type of explosion does this describe?

A   A confined vapour cloud explosion.

B   A secondary explosion.

C   A boiling liquid expanding vapour explosion.

D   An unconfined vapour cloud explosion.

Q3. Development of an emergency plan should consider areas that are:

A   on-site only.

B   either on-site or off-site.

C   off-site only.

D   on-site and off-site.

Practice questions and references

Q4. Which is the preferred fire extinguishing media in a typical process control room?

A   Chemical powder.

B   Foam deluge.

C   Carbon dioxide.

D   Water deluge.

Q5. In processes that involve combustible dusts, why is it especially important to maintain good housekeeping?

A   Dust can build up on a variety of flat and irregular surfaces which can spontaneously ignite.

B   Dust on surfaces can be disturbed by a primary explosion causing a larger secondary explosion.

C   Dust build up on surfaces can be clearly seen by visitors and gives a poor image of the company.

D   Dust will adversely affect limit sensors and proximity switches causing them to malfunction.

Q6. Flammable liquid leaked from a storage vessel into the bund which surrounded it. The liquid began to fill the bund. Liquid also began to leak through cracks in the bund and flow towards a faulty electrical pump usually used to empty the bund of rain water.

Within minutes the entire bund was on fire, taking several hours to extinguish. What is the best description of this type of fire?

A   Jet fire.

B   Pool fire.

C   Flash fire.

D   Secondary fire.

Notes

Element 4 answers: Q1 - B; Q2 - C; Q3 - D; Q4 - C; Q5 - B; Q6 - B.

Element 4 **Fire and explosion protection**

129

Notes